Don Price is one of the most godl disciplined leaders that I have ever met the stories and principles that have sh inspired, encouraged and challenged passion for the development of godly character shines through. I would encourage anyone who is serious about discipleship and spiritual formation to read it, and the application of the principles contained within will lay a strong foundation for enduring ministry for Jesus.

Ian King
Leader of Restore Community Churches

The most engaging parts of Being Real are the personal anecdotes. The pithy, finely honed phrases of discipling truth are both winsome and very helpful. When these two aspects combine (wisdom simply expressed and real-life examples) it is deeply transformative and has real impact.

I'm struck by the integrity of your writing – that you speak and teach on humility while at the same time demonstrating it. There is a thorough convergence between the man I know and the man portrayed here.

Catherine Wait
Restore Kids, Restore Community Church

'Spirit is thicker than blood' – Don Price has exemplified the very essence of this in his own words in this book. You will be challenged, encouraged, inspired, and left in awe of what God can achieve in a yielded vessel. I pray the words 'Spirit is thicker than blood' will also change the trajectory of your life forever, as it did mine.

Paul Henry
Architect

Being Real discipled me and has left a deep impression on my life! A must-read for anyone who desires to know God authentically. Don shares relevant events of his life which are truly impacting. I'm astounded by the way he connects with his family and friends and humbled by his decision to serve because he wants to. Each chapter left me reflecting on the unassuming ways in which God works in our lives.

Vanessa Cariba
Marketing Manager

Being Real made me stop and reflect on my own life and journey of faith. It was as if God was talking to me personally. My wife and I were particularly touched by the stories of living by faith, adoption and forgiveness. It gave us a glimpse into lives authentically lived in dependence on God, inspired by Jesus, soaked in prayer, guided by faith, and driven by obedience.

Neil Porter
Civil Engineer

God let me experience His fatherly love and acceptance through Don. It was a healing force in my own journey as I no longer had a father of my own. I was a neighbour to the Price family for nine years. An atmosphere of peace and loving harmony always filled their home despite them having distinct and unique personalities. I have wanted to emulate that in my own young family and wished that Don had written a book so that I could uncover some of the keys to their lifestyle.

Needless to say, Being Real is a treasure to me! Not only is it a testament to God's faithfulness to the Price family over many years, it is a practical account of how Don and Cecilia have appropriated biblical truth and principles into their lives. The truths presented are refreshingly simple in a not-so-simple modern world and the impact on my life has been profound. It makes me hunger for a deeper relationship with God and encourages me to discover more fully my own unique calling.

Lani Swart
Audiologist

'Simple truth simply spoken' Throughout this book Don weaves the truth of Father God's sovereign love and power. This is no textbook of theory and Christian theology, it's the story of a real life and real events. The story of an ordinary person who lives his life with an extraordinary God. Don says that he wishes that he could describe God to us, he has. God's grace, love and power can be seen in every page of Being Real.

Steve Hale
Head Teacher

BEING REAL

Simple Truth Simply Spoken

BEING REAL

Simple Truth Simply Spoken

A Journey of Discipleship

Don Price

Independently Published by

Donovan J Price

United Kingdom

donovanjprice@gmail.com

Edited by

Catherine Wait

ISBN: 978-1-9997953-0-6

e-ISBN: 978-1-9997953-1-3

A CIP catalogue record of this book is available from the British Library.

First edition 2018

I dedicate these memoirs, intertwined with the principles we learnt together, to my darling wife Cecilia and to our four precious children Cindy-Joy, John, Donovan and David.

It is as much their story as mine.

Foreword

Don and Cecilia Price are legends! I mean this in the literal sense of the word. Everywhere in the world I meet people and leaders of note who know Don and Cecilia. They always respond with a predictable smile and a nod of appreciation when their names are introduced into the conversation, reflecting authentic Kingdom living. Leana and I have shared life and ministry with them over an extended period and regard them highly.

I want to congratulate Don on taking the time to write this book, it will unquestionably be an inspiration to many. Their story as a family, their journey of faith, and the amazing principles they have chosen to frame their lives by, will bless many a reader. Don and I were colleagues in ministry for many years. I therefore have to share a few remarks on the man. These are some of the impressions as I reflect on his life.

Humility - I remember meeting Don in Kempton Park towards the middle of the 1980s. He and his family were members of the Emmanuel Church where I was the Youth Pastor. I was also overseeing the small groups in the church and was responsible for the training of new leaders. And who signs up - Don Price, Mr Discipleship himself – I could not believe the ease and humility that Don subjected himself to my lightweight training course at that time! This humility has been the trademark of his life during all the years I had the privilege of being associated with him!

Fathering - Don has entrenched wisdom principles into his life. He knows, speaks and lives according to life-giving principles. They are like massive spotlights in his life creating very little space for uncertainty which brings unbelievable stability and trust where both Don and Cecilia are involved. This has especially become evident with the next generation as they became surrogate parents to the many young South Africans in the London context.

Pioneering Spirit - I salute Don and Cecilia on behalf of the Doxa Deo family for their brave and selfless commitment to pioneer church-plant in the city of London. This paved the way for the ministry of Doxa Deo to take root in the city. Don is a man of faith and conviction, whose commitment within YWAM and Doxa Deo has released many others to now stand on his shoulders – his legacy lives on.

On this point, one of the major values in the Doxa Deo Family is our commitment to engagement in the eight 'spheres of influence' in society. Few people know that that was forged through the contribution of Don at a leadership level in Doxa Deo. He helped us grasp, define and embrace the concept of the Gospel of the Kingdom. It has not only become standard practice in Doxa Deo but is also fast becoming the strategy of churches all over the world. You have a proud legacy Don!

Enjoy this book – may it inspire and challenge you – and to Don and Cecilia, may the years ahead be grace filled, and evident of Gods favour on all you do.

Alan Platt
Leader of Doxa Deo and City Changers Movement

Preface

The quest of my life is to be real, to discover a freedom on the one hand to be myself and live out my unique design, while on the other hand to walk in integrity so that Jesus can be His own great glorious self through me. A few years ago, as I started reflecting on the period of forty years in full-time Christian service, I was prompted to 'steward the journey' and to document some of the lessons learned on the way. My initial thought was to pass the principles on to my children and grandchildren at least, but was soon inspired to write for a much wider audience. These pages will relate that journey. It has been a journey of liberation from the trappings of tradition and legalism, from inferiority and the fear of man. It has been a journey discovering simple principles to live by. It is also a story of God's incredible faithfulness.

One of the most common affirmations that I have received during these more than forty years of ministry has been related to the simplicity of the truth taught and the simplicity of the presentations given. Consequently, the subtitle of this collage of memoirs: Simple Truth Simply Spoken.

Biographies are written about prominent people, with authors choosing to capture their greatness. People like me are left to write about themselves. I write these thoughts with no claim whatsoever to greatness. I do write with deep compulsion, however, convinced that the lessons I have learnt, some of them the hard way, will be helpful to others who are open to learn.

What a rich treasure is the storehouse of memories, some are pleasant and some are very painful. You wish you could go back and rewrite the history of some of the unpleasant and disappointing chapters of your life, but you can't. It is water under the bridge. You also wish you could have tarried a little longer at the more pleasant moments, but you can't either - time marches on relentlessly.

I have endeavoured to explore the storehouse of my experiences to piece together some thoughts that I trust speak of God's goodness and faithfulness. References to myself and to my family are deliberate and intentional to reflect God's journey of grace with us. To Him be all the glory!

The Price family can be traced back to King Rhys, the great king of South Wales in the second century. I have found two different mottos associated with the Price family crest. The one is Vita Brevis, Gloria Aeterna, which means 'Life is short, but glory is eternal.' This was mostly associated with going to war but I will take the deeper meaning, as we are primarily eternal beings having a short human experience.

The other ancient motto for the Price family is Auxilium Muem a Domino, meaning 'My help is from the Lord.' My help has certainly been from the Lord and for that I am eternally grateful.

Donovan John Price

TABLE OF CONTENTS

Author's Introduction

This is a brief overview of Cecilia and my lives and a short summary of the last forty-four years (1974-2017) in full time Christian ministry.

We both grew up in Edenvale, on the eastern outskirts of Johannesburg in South Africa. Cecilia's mother tongue is Afrikaans while mine was English. She is the firstborn of seven children – one brother and five sisters. I am the eldest of three, having two sisters. We both came from very stable and settled families. I, for example, only attended two schools - Eastleigh Primary School and Edenvale English Medium High School - in my hometown while Cecilia only attended three schools.

We both committed our lives to Christ at an early age and attended a Pentecostal church called The Apostolic Faith Mission (AFM), one of the bigger denominations in South Africa. Being involved in all the aspects of church life was very central to our upbringing.

I played both cricket and soccer (football) at primary and high school. Cecilia was an excellent track and field athlete and enjoyed playing netball for her schools. We both enjoyed the privilege of being Head Boy and Head Girl respectively during our final year at school.

Cecilia and I were married on 5 February 1972. I was still studying B.Sc. Civil Engineering at the University of Witwatersrand and she was working as a private secretary in the legal department of the South African Broadcasting Corporation (SABC). I never did go on to register as a professional Civil Engineer.

We have four children. Cindy-Joy was born in November 1980, John and Donovan in November 1983 and David in January 1989. We also have four grandchildren - Luke and Jonathan to Cindy and Jeff Wiseman and Joshua and Ava to John and Brenda Price.

In 1974 Cecilia and I attended a School of Evangelism (SOE) with Youth with a Mission (YWAM) in Lausanne, Switzerland. Initially the idea was to take a break from our jobs to receive some equipping in 'getting to know God so that we could make him known' and then to return to our careers. However, we went on to work in YWAM for twenty-five years, which included two years of transition into local church ministry.

In YWAM we had the privilege of leading a School of Evangelism in what was then Rhodesia, (now Zimbabwe); help pioneer the training programmes in South Africa; establish a training base in Namibia and initiate YWAM in the Western Cape, South Africa. I served as a Base Leader, National Director and Southern Africa Area Director of YWAM. I have had the privilege to minister in various ways, including numerous opportunities with Mercy Ships, in fifty-six different countries. I also had the joy of being part of initiating Mercy Air in Southern Africa and seeing it established as a viable aviation ministry by some incredible aviation pioneers.

In January 1997 we transitioned into local church ministry by joining the ministry team of the Doxa Deo Church in Pretoria. The vision of Doxa Deo is to see cities transformed by the Glory of God to places where Jesus reigns and to mobilise 'city changers' to establish the Kingdom of God in every sphere of influence in society. Initially, I was involved in co-ordinating the mission projects of the church but gradually got more involved in church life including being on the pioneering team of the Inner-City Campus in Pretoria as an 'urban missionary'.

In March 2004 Cecilia and I were sent to London to plant a Doxa Deo church with the many graduate young people from our church who were migrating to the United Kingdom on a two-year working holiday visa. Doxa Deo London was officially launched in September 2004 with about 200 people in attendance and Alan Platt, the visionary leader and founder of Doxa Deo, presiding.

In 2006 the bulk of the church moved to Stratford in the north-east of the city while we kept meeting on Sunday afternoons with a smaller group in south-west London until it became the Raynes Park Campus in 2008, and later the Wimbledon Campus.

I served on the core leadership team of Doxa Deo (in the latter years referred to as the Apostolic Empowerment Team or AET) for sixteen years. Alan Platt, encouraged us to be looking out for kingdom relationships that God might be leading us into. On 16 December 2012, we entered into a partnership with Restore Community Church by joining the Doxa Deo Loughton congregation with the Restore congregation in Loughton. Alan Platt officiated at this historic event. Doxa Deo London continued as a separate congregation in South West London.

Restore Community Church, led by Ian and Chris King, is now in an informal friendship relationship with the international Doxa Deo family of churches. We relate specifically to the English-speaking

Parkview Congregation in Tshwane, South Africa and Popup - People Upliftment Project, a skills development programme.

At the time of writing I am the Pastoral Leader of Restore Community Church in Loughton, London. It is a multi-cultural, multi-national and multi-generational congregation of approximately 350 adults and 150 children with many more people being served and impacted by the influence of the church in the broader community. We are also engaged and integrally involved with 'Churches Together' in Loughton where we enjoy an incredibly high level of unity and mutual trust.

Cecilia and I are determined to continue living by faith and to trust God irrevocably for our future. We look forward to the unfolding of the next season of our lives and anticipate it to be more significant than anything that has gone before - as an enduring testimony to the faithfulness of God.

December 2017

Chapter 1
The Point of No Return

Then Jesus told his disciples, 'If anyone would come after me,
he must deny himself and take up his cross and follow me.
For whoever wants to save his life will lose it,
but whoever loses his life for me will find it.'
Matthew 16:24,25

He is no fool who gives what he cannot keep
to gain what he cannot lose.
Jim Elliot

On our wedding day on 4 February 1972 Cecilia looked me in the eyes and serenaded me with the hymn Each for the other and both for the Lord. Little did we know how prophetic that would be.

The Journey

In mid-1973 we met a team from Youth with a Mission (YWAM) touring South Africa. They were reporting on the International Christian outreach that took place during the ill-fated Munich Olympic Games the previous year. Seventy South Africans had been amongst the 1000 participants and the team were reporting back to their sending churches and promoting the opportunities for training and service in YWAM. We were intrigued by their testimonies of faith and mission exploits and learnt from them that the motto of YWAM was 'To know God and make Him known.' That struck a chord in our hearts. We realised then that we did not know God well enough to make Him known. In our church tradition we had been effectively evangelized as children, teenagers and young adults but never effectively trained or discipled in the practicalities of living the Christian life.

That chance meeting with the YWAM team proved to be a pivotal point that would change the course of our entire lives. We decided to take a break from our respective career paths to attend a training program with YWAM. It led to a hectic and exciting few months of preparation. We prayed to understand the will of God. We sought counsel and advice from family and friends and submitted our guidance to our church leadership. We changed plans and organised our finances. On 1 January 1974 we were in Lausanne, Switzerland to attend the School of Evangelism under the leadership of Loren and Darlene Cunningham, the founders of YWAM. The school lasted eight months. We never anticipated that the short break would develop into a lifetime of involvement in missions and church work.

The School of Evangelism (SOE) was divided into three phases: the Messenger, the Message, and the Methods of evangelism. During the Messenger stage we found the training deeply enriching and exceptionally life-changing. We were taught how to hear God's voice for ourselves; to live with a clear conscience; to have an effective prayer and devotional life; and we learnt about the Nature and Character of God. We were often moved to tears by the transformational power of the Word of God in our lives. Cecilia and I both regretted not having had this powerful discipleship training earlier in our Christian walk.

The richness of the SOE model of training was that we had a different speaker for each of the twelve weeks. They were all seasoned ministers in their respective fields and shared from many years of experience. The idea was that we could learn in one week what had taken them years and sometimes decades to learn, if we were willing to internalise the teaching and make the principles our own.

One Monday morning a tall, scrawny man with shoulder- length hair, a long beard and prominent cheek bones walked into the lecture room. He was dressed in off-white Afghan robes. I thought to myself, 'Wow! This guy is ugly.' Floyd McClung was our teacher for that week. He had come from Kabul, Afghanistan where he and his wife Sally were running a rescue center for Western young people in search of meaning, on the hippie trail to the East. This gentle giant started teaching us with a passion on his love for Jesus and God's love for the people of the world. We learnt from Floyd that: 'People don't care how much you know until they know how much you care.' By the end of the week I had to swallow my sentiments and acknowledge that Floyd was the person most like Jesus I had ever met. He went on to have a major mentoring influence in my life both through personal interaction and working together on a leadership team as well as through his prolific teachings and writing.

We were thoroughly blessed and genuinely encouraged by the teaching and testimonies of our speakers week after week. We were convinced that it was possible to live a victorious Christian life and to rightly represent Jesus here on earth. This all had a profound impact on our journey of discipleship.

During this time I was deeply challenged by the notion portrayed in the Bible that we were to obey and 'fear the LORD our God, for our good always' (Deuteronomy 6:24 NKJV). And the conclusion that the book of Ecclesiastes comes to that the whole duty of mankind is to

'Fear God and keep his commandments' (12:13). Also the challenge from Jesus Himself, 'If you love me, keep my commands' (John 14:15).

After our wedding day, the next most significant moment in my life was when Cecilia and I stood hand in hand before God to make the following commitment: 'Lord you can take our lives and do with our lives whatever you want to. The answer will always be yes as long as you give us the assurance that it is your will.' That poignant moment is still ingrained in my memory. We had come to our 'point of no return'.

It was February 1974. We were responding to a lecture by Joy Dawson during our School of Evangelism in Lausanne on the Lordship of Christ. We made that commitment simply on the realisation first, that God loved us immensely and, secondly, that He was a lot cleverer and wiser than us. We believed that God wanted the best for our lives and that He also knew exactly what that was. Our logic told us that to commit to the will of God for our lives was the most intelligent thing to do. Not to obey God, not to follow His agenda for our lives would be ill-advised, foolish and unintelligent.

Within months of coming to this place of total surrender we had the privilege of embarking on a three-month field trip through the Middle East and Eastern Europe, that tracked some of the missionary routes of Paul the Apostle. We visited places such as Rome, Corinth, Philippi, and Thessalonica and studied the appropriate letters to the New Testament churches in these places. As we stood on the Acropolis in Athens we reflected on Paul's apologetic sermon to the Greeks about the unknown god they worshipped. In Israel, we reflected on the servant leadership of Jesus and His discipleship methods. We sat on the rolling hills of the shores of the Sea of Galilee and received teaching on Jesus' Sermon on the Mount, reflecting that He would have taught His disciples the same things in a similar setting. It was very refreshing and spiritually enriching.

We walked the cobblestone streets of the old walled city, retracing the footsteps of Jesus. Dozens of little kids thronged the streets and ran by. My heart went out to them. In my mind's eye I saw Jesus sitting on the side of the road, gathering the little children around him and blessing them. So I started doing that. I would stop children running past, look them in the eyes, smile, lay my hands on them, and bless them in the name of Jesus. Very soon children would be crowding around me. I would pray over them in the Spirit; claim them to have an influence in the Nations; resist the agenda of the evil one over their lives; and release the blessings of God on them.

As we travelled in Turkey and visited the cities and the sites of the Seven Churches of Revelations crowds of children would gather around the YWAMers as they sang and played on their guitars. I would stride into the crowd and bless as many children as I could lay my hands on. A spark was lit in my heart. A longing developed that one day I would have children of my own that I could bless, that I could communicate with, that I could pour my life into, and that I could father.

Turkey was also very challenging as it exposed us to the sober realities of the Mission task. Amongst the 50 million inhabitants of Turkey then, there were very few known Turkish believers. This was the geographic area of the New Testament church and the amphitheatre of the Acts of the Apostles. Biblical cities such as Antioch – called the 'cradle of Christianity' - and Tarsus as well as Ephesus and the other cities of the 'Seven Churches of Revelations' were all in modern day Turkey. And now there was hardly a remnant of Christianity left. That deeply challenged us. A seed of concern was planted in our hearts for the nations and the unreached peoples of the world.

During our time in Turkey we prepared for a visit behind the so-called Iron Curtain. The term Iron Curtain was coined by Winston Churchill in World War II for the Eastern Bloc Soviet states that had isolated themselves from Western influence.

It seemed impossible that we as South Africans would be able to get visas for these supposed closed countries. On page five of our original passports is this statement: 'THIS PASSPORT IS VALID FOR ALL COUNTRIES EXCEPT: Albania, Bulgaria, China (Peking), Cuba, Czechoslovakia, East Germany, Hungary, Mongolia, North Korea, Poland, Romania, The USSR, North Vietnam, UNLESS OTHERWISE ENDORSED.'

A few pages further there are Bulgarian and Romanian visas as a testimony to God's miraculous provision. Even though we were unable to obtain a visa for The USSR and had to travel back to Western Europe through Yugoslavia while the rest of our group visited Russia, God was teaching us to trust Him in impossible situations. The miraculous provision of the visas and these three weeks in Bulgaria, Romania and Yugoslavia would irrevocably change our lives.

In these communist countries we were exposed to the cost of discipleship and challenged to a more radical surrender of our lives to Christ. We had the awesome privilege of meeting true believers who were totally committed to Christ and who were willing to lay down their lives for Him. This, and the blind commitment of young communists to the cause of world communism, made a profound impact on us.

Every evening, while camped on the outskirts of Sofia the capital of Bulgaria, we would listen to the reports of people who had gone out secretly that day to contact believers and to deliver Bibles and Christian books. I had hoped that we would be given that privilege but still had some apprehension when our group leader gave us a bag of Bibles and a map of the city with instructions to make two deliveries the next day.

It was with some trepidation that Cecilia and I alighted from the taxi and stepped into the park that we had identified on our map as a point of reference. There was a policeman patrolling the area. Although we obviously stood out as foreign tourists we wanted to avoid being questioned at all cost. Apart from not wanting the Bibles to be confiscated we especially wanted to avoid being followed for fear of our contact being exposed and prejudiced. We sat down on a nearby park bench, prayed, took out some sandwiches and tried to act as naturally and casually as possible - just two lovebirds having lunch in the park. We had some difficulty orientating ourselves as our map was in English but all the street signs were in Bulgarian and written in their Cyrillic script.

In order not to attract too much attention and be as vigilant as possible I had Cecilia carry the bag of Bibles and books to pretend that it was just a picnic bag. We slipped down a side street when the policeman was on the other side of the park. A few blocks down we located the address of our first contact. She was the widow of a Baptist pastor. It seemed like forever before our gentle knocking was answered and the door slowly creaked open. We greeted the middle-aged lady with the appropriate password that we had been given. She showed no emotion and did not say a word as she beckoned us inside and ushered us up a flight of stairs into a small room, closing the door on us. She left us alone in that small living room for what again felt like an age, before returning.

As circumspectly as possible we shared with her that we were students from South Africa who loved the Lord Jesus and were delighted to fellowship with her. It took some time for her to thaw and to warm to us. As our spirits witnessed together she saw that she could trust us and began to share her heart openly. She shared how she had typed out portions of the New Testament on an old typewriter and multiplied them on an equally archaic Gestetner machine. She was working on translating a Bible commentary from German into Bulgarian. A state-appointed minister conducted a service in their church one Sunday per month. Three passionately committed students conducted services regularly in the so-called underground church on the other Sundays. She testified to revival amongst the youth although it was officially illegal for anyone under the age of eighteen to attend church. She told us of Bible study groups that she was conducting and of a lady that had come to know the Lord Jesus just that week.

She had promised the new convert that she would try and find her a New Testament. We were then able to place a half dozen or so Bibles and as many Christian books on the table. The emotion of that moment is unforgettable! She was dumbfounded and deeply appreciative. She assigned a value to the printed 'Word of God' more than we had experienced before. Words cannot express the imprint and impact of those few seconds on our spirits. We had seen the metamorphosis of a cautious, somewhat timid and fearful lady into a precious sister in the Lord. Spirit truly transcends nationality, language and culture. Spiritual bonds are stronger than those of race, generation or denomination. We were family!

After rejoicing together and enjoying a bowl of the biggest and best strawberries we had ever seen in our lives, she prayed for us. I know that my mother has often prayed for my siblings and me throughout her life. This saint's prayer for us was at least on par with the most fervent loving prayers of a concerned mother for her vulnerable children. Her prayer for us was filled with warmth, empathy, concern, and emotion. We felt humbled and utterly blessed.

We walked away from that humble abode in the suburbs of Sofia that mid-summer afternoon deeply challenged. We realised that in South Africa it was easy to call oneself a Christian. There was no price to pay, no real persecution. But here behind the Iron Curtain, because of the cost involved to call yourself a Christian, you had to sincerely mean it. You were truly committed.

Because our tour through Eastern Europe was registered as a 'School of Languages and Culture' we were obliged to visit college and university campuses as students. As a group, we met students from the Communist Youth League who were radically sold out to the cause of world communism. They challenged us with the slogan 'We are ragged and we are poor but we are changing the world.' They were willing to sacrifice everything for their cause: give up careers and relationships; go without money; and leave home. They were prepared to sacrifice everything.

This blind commitment to the cause of communism by these young people confronted and deeply challenged us. But it was the radical, deep-seated commitment to Christ of Christians, being persecuted for their faith in these repressive states that reinforced our resolve to a life of total surrender to the loving cause of Christ. His was a cause not only worth living for but also worth dying for. The point of no return had been firmly established in our lives. It was no longer negotiable: Jesus was to be the Lord of our entire life.

oOo

Chapter 2
Spirit is Thicker than Blood

For you did not receive the spirit of bondage again to fear,
but you received the Spirit of adoption by whom we cry out,
'Abba, Father'. The Spirit Himself bears witness with our
spirit that we are the children of God.
Romans 8:15,16 (NKJV)

The Gospel is not a picture of adoption,
adoption is a picture of the Gospel.
John Piper

My wife Cecilia weighed heavily on my heart and my emotions were in turmoil as I negotiated the winding track into Blantyre, Malawi. The air was hot and dusty and there was a heavy atmosphere in the car. My passengers were a pastor from Rhodesia (now Zimbabwe) and a friend, Wade Robertson. I had promised that I would take the pastor to a conference in Blantyre while Wade and I were going to investigate the possibilities of a YWAM field trip through Mozambique and Malawi.

It was February 1975 and only hours before I had stood by Cecilia's bedside in the recovery room of the Salisbury Hospital in the capital city of Rhodesia. I had intended to wait for her to recover from the anaesthetic of, what I expected to be, minor surgery and then leave on the mission expedition to Mozambique and Malawi. I needed to leave within the hour to fulfil my commitment to the pastor to get him to the conference by nightfall.

The surgery had taken longer than expected and had not been minor. There had been complications. Several growths had been removed from the lining of her womb as well as one ovary and a fallopian tube. The remaining ovary was susceptible to bleeding and the fallopian tube was deformed. It was a condition called endometriosis. I listened distraught as the surgeon informed me that there might be complications with conception in the future. I was completely taken aback. I had obviously been naïve with regards to my wife's true gynaecological condition. I had no idea it was that bad. We had just celebrated our third wedding anniversary.

I was shocked at the sight of my wife and torn between wanting to be with her and support her and the need to leave to fulfil my responsibility towards the pastor. What should I do? My mind was racing and my heart was pounding when Cecilia finally woke up from the anaesthetic. After a brief conversation, I told her I loved her, kissed her goodbye, and with a very heavy heart left her for the longest five days of my life.

As we left the city limits of Salisbury (now Harare) and turned northeast for the 500-kilometre drive through Mozambique to Malawi my mind was preoccupied with Cecilia's medical condition and what had just transpired at the hospital. I soon realised that I had made the wrong decision and should have cancelled the trip.

I had clearly not yet learnt to prioritise. This was our first year in missions. We had been taught the priority: God first, family second, and then ministry third. Here I was torn between my responsibility to my precious wife and a ministry commitment. I had not foreseen the need to change my commitment in the light of my wife's physical condition. I felt terribly embarrassed and insecure at this immaturity. I had a lot to learn. I realised that I would have to ask more questions, make sure of all the facts, not presume anything, and be much more sensitive to the needs of those around me. I would also have to rely more heavily on the guidance of the Holy Spirit in setting priorities and making decisions. It was a deeply humbling experience.

A few hours into the journey I remembered that it was almost a year to the day since we had come to our 'point of no return' in Switzerland.

That commitment had brought us to Rhodesia. We had come to this land-locked African nation less than nine months later at the request of Loren Cunningham the founder of YWAM and in obedience to what we believed to be the call of God upon our lives. Within months of arriving in Rhodesia we had rented a venue, organized speakers and started a School of Evangelism (SOE) with forty students from twelve nations. God had honoured our small steps of obedience and little faith. We were discovering Him as a faithful and miraculous God. This trip to Malawi and Mozambique was to put plans in place for a Southern Africa fieldtrip for the SOE students.

Cecilia's recollection of those five days of being separated from one another is that she was well cared for by the medical professionals and visited by friends. She was pre-occupied with recovering from the anaesthetic and the surgery and not thinking of my mission expedition.

It was only at the post-op visit with the surgeon that the possibility of never being able to conceive hit us. During the ensuing months and years Cecilia and I were able to work through the disappointing prospect of maybe never being parents. Our trust in God and personal relationship with him was the predominant sustaining factor. We grew ever closer to one another.

Cecilia and I had been married for seven years when we started contemplating the possibility of adoption. Although we were fulfilled in our ministry, enjoyed our marriage, and loved one another dearly, we felt the increasing need to be parents. There was a growing desire in our hearts to share our love for each other with children of our own, and to invest our lives in them.

We had many dear friends and family who encouraged us that we would be good parents. Among them were friends who had adopted three children before they, as parents, had become Christians. They only later discovered all the redeeming principles to be applied in family life. After hearing our story they strongly encouraged us to start the adoption process without delay. They thought that with all the good Christian principles we had been exposed to we would make excellent adopters. Within days we started making enquiries and researching the possibility of adoption.

Blood Is Thicker Than Water

We also had several friends and some family members with the 'ministry of discouragement'. They tried to dissuade us from considering adoption. Inevitably they would use the cliché 'blood is thicker than water' to challenge us about our ability to love a child not born of us. I was confused. I knew I had a lot of love in my heart for children.

As I prayed about it I remembered walking the cobblestone streets of the old city of Jerusalem for the first time in 1974 and my heart going out to the children running in the streets. I had laid my hands on them and blessed them, seeking to do as I believe Jesus would have done. It was a practice I repeated in countries in the Middle East and Eastern Europe and all over Africa. I felt an affinity for children, but what was this idea of 'blood is thicker than water'? Could I really love a child that was not biologically mine? Did we have to be blood-related to make family work? I didn't know for sure so I was compelled to lean heavily into God to understand the dynamics of adoption.

I asked Him to show me if we were doing the right thing in considering adoption and to give me an understanding of the 'spirit of adoption'. Revelation came in a very normal way. As we were going through the adoption process and being interviewed by social workers the eye-opener came. I was asked the question: 'Whom do you love more than anyone else?' Of course my answer was that I loved Cecilia more than anybody else. How was this possible, since we were not-blood related? I realised I loved her because I wanted to love her. I loved her because she opened her heart and life to me. We loved each other because we had chosen to, because we wanted to.

For the first time in my almost thirty years I experienced God the Father engage me directly and speak into my spirit with as close to an audible voice as I have ever heard: 'Don, that is exactly how I love you. I don't have to; I want to. I choose to love you'.

That's when the penny dropped for me. I realised for the first time in my life that the sovereign, almighty God of the universe actually liked me and that He accepted me and loved me. Not because He had to, but because He wanted to. I had known theoretically and theologically that God is Love but in that moment, it became personal. It was real. It was no longer just in my head but in my heart. God truly loved ME unconditionally.

This revolutionised my relationship with God. I had been taught to reverence and respect God but I had no intimate relationship with Him as a father. In my mind, I had relegated Him to be ruling from a distance, from outside time and space. Suddenly He was in my space. All distance was cancelled. He sought relationship with me as a father with a son.

The Spirit of Adoption

I realised instantly then that the 'spirit of adoption' is simply a spirit of acceptance. It is a spirit that says 'I love you because I want to. I accept you – unconditionally.' To rebut the notion that 'blood is thicker than water' I formulated the concept that 'spirit is thicker than blood' to emphasise that relationship by choice from the heart and the spirit transcends biology and tribal, racial or even natural family ties.

It was only a while later that this passage in Galatians came alive to me as it summarised what I had experienced in my spirit:

But when the fullness of the time had come, God sent forth His Son, born of a woman, born under the law, to redeem those who were under the law, that we might receive the adoption of sons. And because you are sons, God has sent forth the Spirit of His Son into your hearts, crying out, Abba, Father! (Galatians 4:4-6 NKJV).

Once we understand that the reason Jesus came and died on the cross was to restore our identity as children of God, the Spirit of God is released in our hearts whereby we acknowledge Him as our Father and cry out 'Abba Father' or 'daddy Father' from the depth of our being. Our identity as children of God and the security and comfort that comes from that is directly related to our understanding of Him as our Father.

Becoming Parents

It was Tuesday 25 November 1980. We were in Johannesburg. My heart was pounding in my chest and Cecilia and I looked at each other eagerly as the social worker left the room to fetch our baby daughter. After being married for almost nine years we were going to be childless for only a few more minutes. The excitement of the last few days seemed trivial compared to the significance of this moment. It was huge!

Five days earlier, on a Thursday afternoon I walked into our house in Windhoek, Namibia carrying a tray of dirty dishes from our outdoor lunch. I had held the tray in my left hand while answering the phone with my right hand. It was the adoption agency! They had a baby for us! Could we be in Johannesburg on Tuesday? 'Remember to bring a bottle and a change of clothes and your identity documents.' 'Yes! Yes! Yes!' I responded as nonchalantly as possible while trying to catch my breath.

As I replaced the receiver in its cradle Cecilia and her friends, who had been dawdling behind me, stepped into the house. I shared with considerable excitement the news from the adoption agency: they had a baby for us. Cecilia did not believe me! She thought that I was being mischievous and joking with them, and their suspicions were confirmed when I could not tell them if it was a baby boy or girl. In all the excitement I had forgotten to ask. I immediately called back and the agency confirmed that it was a beautiful baby girl.

By now Cecilia was crying with joy and being hugged by equally tearful friends. What a joyous moment!

We thanked God for excellent timing. We had flights booked to Johannesburg for the next day to officiate at the wedding of close friends on the Saturday. We were to make the trip anyway but now we were going for a much greater reason than a friend's wedding. We were going to grow from a family of two to a family of three.

Just five days later and the time had finally arrived! A little bundle was placed into Cecilia's arms and we were left alone to savour this moment of becoming parents. Cindy-Joy was stunningly beautiful. Even at three weeks old her black hair and deep blue eyes were remarkable. She stared into Cecilia's eyes as if to say: 'This is her. I know you. I belong.' They locked eyes for several minutes allowing me to take a few photos. I laid a hand on her head and said: 'Cindy-Joy this sounds funny, I know. I realise that you don't understand what I am saying but I want to speak into your heart and tell you that we love you. You belong to us. You are ours.'

In the Spirit, we knew a bonding had taken place. We were not strangers to each other. Two years of prayer and preparation, of releasing our love and acceptance in the Spirit, had paid off. We knew we were family. Spirit truly is thicker than blood.

Round Two

Three years and four months later almost the same scenario repeated itself. We were living in Cape Town at the time. At about 2 pm on a Thursday afternoon we got a call from the adoption agency. The social worker told me that they had decided to place twin boys with us. She asked if we could be in Johannesburg four days later to receive them. There was a conflict of dates! I was leaving on the Saturday for three weeks to attend a missions conference in Cyprus and then a time of ministry in the UK and Ireland. We quickly resolved the issue and agreed to be in Johannesburg, a good 1200km away, at 8am the next morning to welcome the boys into our family.

Cecilia overheard me negotiating with the social worker on the phone and immediately started getting excited. As I put the receiver back in its cradle she jumped up and asked me with considerable emotion 'Is it a boy or a girl?' (Remember the first time I had forgotten to ask.) I suggested she sit down and then with as much theatrical effect as I could muster I told her 'Twins! Two boys!' Cecilia jumped up and down in delight, almost hitting the low ceiling and hugging a guest that had enjoyed lunch with us. I noticed three-year-old Cindy-Joy standing off to the side looking a little bewildered by all the commotion. Kneeling beside her and putting an arm around her I said, 'Cindy-Joy we have just heard that you are going to get two baby brothers. Do you see how happy Mommy is? Well, she was just as happy when we got the news about you.' I believe that this helped her to understand her own story and to reinforce our love for and acceptance of her. She was animated by all the excitement in the room and was beaming at the prospect of being the older sister to twin brothers.

We again thanked God for the excellent timing. At this stage Cecilia and I were pioneering the work of YWAM in the Western Cape. Just a week previously we had moved into a house in Cape Town from Rawsonville where we had been living temporarily with friends on a beautiful wine farm. When we moved, Cecilia felt that we needed to allocate a baby room in the new house. We duly did, not knowing that the twins had already been born and we were going to need it so soon.

On 9 March 1984 Cindy-Joy joined Cecilia and me as we welcomed John Walter and Donovan John into our hearts and lives. It was a special moment to be given the boys and be left alone for an hour or so of bonding as a new family of five. It is our opinion (biased of course) that they felt immediately at home and knew in their spirits that they belonged with us. Our prayers had been answered.

The Sequel

We learnt an incredible amount about the unconditional love and acceptance of God and His huge Father heart towards us through the adoption process and becoming adoptive parents ourselves. We wouldn't want it any other way. Both Cecilia and I felt extremely fortunate and honoured by having our own, adorable, adopted children. We were entirely surrendered to the plan and will of God for us as a family. We found it easy to celebrate with friends and colleagues when they announced that they were pregnant. I remember Alan and Leana Platt being deeply touched when we prayed with them and blessed their unborn child. We were entirely content as a family of five and not anticipating any more children. But God had other plans.

On Saturday 14 May 1988 Cecilia shared with me that she thought she might be pregnant. I shrugged off the possibility. After all, what's the big deal in missing one 'cycle' in seventeen years of marriage? I dismissed the idea, rolled over and fell soundly asleep. When I awoke in the morning Cecilia was already up and about and getting breakfast ready for the family. In the bathroom I was confronted with a plastic device. There was a perfect circle on a little slide. I called out to Cecilia, 'What does it mean if it forms a circle?' 'That means I'm positively pregnant!' came the ecstatic reply from the kitchen. In a panic, I grabbed the instructions to ensure that the directions had been followed religiously. They had! It seemed that my wife, six weeks from her thirty seventh birthday, was pregnant.

I felt a rush of mixed feelings. I didn't know what to think. Why was I not overjoyed at the news? I knew it was a miracle. I should be elated. But I wasn't. My emotions were in turmoil.

I find it difficult at the best of times to label my emotions, let alone at such an extraordinary moment. So early that autumn Sunday morning I went for a walk under the jacaranda trees in the streets of suburban Pretoria to talk to God.

I felt encouraged and deeply humbled by the fact that Cecilia was pregnant. We must have been doing something right with the first three children for God to want to entrust us with a fourth child. If God saw fit to heal Cecilia or cause her to conceive miraculously, who was I to argue? I expressed as much to God. I even wondered if I had anything to do with it. But, why were my emotions in such turmoil? God started ministering to me.

I experienced living through the whole adoption process in a few moments. God reminded me of our longing and anticipation to be parents. Of the lengthy period of being scrutinised as adopters. In an instant I saw the investment of time, emotional energy, and prayer in creating a cocoon of love and acceptance for our adopted children to be conceived into. I loved and carried them in my heart long before they were born. I now felt threatened by the current development. I had invested so much to make the adoption process as harmonious as possible that I now felt threatened that a biological child would rob me of my love for our gorgeous adopted children.

As I walked I felt God affirm me for my deep love for our three children and the investment Cecilia and I had made to counter any possibility of them feeling rejected. He started ministering my own sermon back to me! Wherever I had travelled and had the opportunity to teach I would allude to our story and refer to the concept that 'Spirit is thicker than blood'. I instantly realised that I needed to apply the same principle to the child that Cecilia was carrying. I had to open my heart to adopt and accept our biological child as much as I did the other three. So I unreservedly did. From that day onwards we had four adopted children. They are all four ours, three legally and one biologically and they are all passionately adopted by choice.

Breaking the News to the Family

At this time we were living in a YWAM community of about 200 people and I knew that we would have to break the news of the pregnancy as circumspectly as possible. I didn't want the community to hear from the children or the children to hear from anyone else other than us.

I briefly summarised our family story as we sat around the dining room table and then turned to eight-year-old Cindy-Joy on my right and asked, 'Cindy do you think you have enough room in your heart to adopt another brother or sister?' She immediately said that she did. I asked the twins, then five years old, a similar question and they affirmed that they had love for another brother or sister. I specifically asked Cecilia if she could open her heart to adopt another baby and she said she could. I acknowledged that I thought I had enough room in my heart for many more children. I then declared that all five of us were going to have to open our hearts and home to adopt another little boy or girl because 'Mommy has a baby in her tummy'.

The kids were absolutely elated. Cindy-Joy immediately said that she hoped it was a little sister and starting rattling off some girls' names. The boys argued that they would rather have a baby brother and suggested we put a third bunk above their double bunk and immediately starting debating who was going to sleep on what level!

On 3 January 1989, our fourth child David Jonathan was born and adopted into our family. It is our experience that there has been no rivalry, competition or jealousy amongst the siblings with regards to their identity. Little brother David was just as much adopted as the other three. They adopted him with the same spirit of love and acceptance that they had experienced as they were received into our lives. That's the spirit of adoption – unconditional acceptance.

On the twins' sixteenth birthday Donovan came to me and simply said: 'Dad I want you to know that I adopt you as my father'. I immediately knew what he was saying. We both knew that he had a biological father out there somewhere, but he was affirming, 'That's OK. I accept you as my dad'. That's the spirit of adoption.

For those who have been wondering about loving a child not born of them as opposed to one that is, let me assure you: it is the same. A child is a child! The love is equally deep and heartfelt, intense and overwhelming, astonishing and amazing.

Calling all Parents

I now encourage all parents to 'adopt' their children. Not in the sense of going to an agency to sign documents but in the 'spirit of adoption', a conscious choice to love and accept. If you bring children into this world you are obligated to care for them. You have a responsibility to feed them, to clothe them, to make sure that they are educated. You MUST do it. But it makes a colossal difference if you do it because you WANT to. It is simply the heart attitude or 'spirit' that makes all the difference.

The spirit of adoption is fundamentally a spirit of love and acceptance, a choice to love unconditionally. You can love and accept anybody if you really want to just as God unconditionally loves and accepts us.

oOo

Chapter 3
The Father Heart of God

Then the world will know that you sent me and have loved them even as you have loved me.
John 17:23b

God reveals Himself in the Bible as a gentle forgiving Father, intimately involved with each and every detail of our lives. It is not only a beautiful picture, but a true one.
John Dawson

I most definitely love our three adopted children as much as I love our biological son. I am only a normal human being and an imperfect father. If I am able to do so then how much more must the perfect heavenly Father be able to love and accept us, His adopted children, as much as He loves his own son, Jesus.

I started teaching on the Fatherhood of God in the late 1970s whenever I had the opportunity to preach or share anywhere. But it was only after our experience with adoption and personally encountering God the Father's unconditional love for me that I could share not just from my head but also from my heart and emotions – hence the Father Heart of God.

One of the major factors influencing our perception of God the Father is our relationship with our own fathers.

My Dad

My Dad, John Walter Price, was born in 1925 and passed away in 2009, aged eighty-four, within days of being diagnosed with liver cancer. He was an astute and responsible man. He was diligent, hard working and a good steward of his resources and thus provided well for the family. An abiding lesson I learnt from him was to live within your means, to stay out of debt, and to be financially responsible.

Once when I was about ten years old we were driving home from church one Sunday afternoon and Dad pulled over on the side of the road and asked me to buy a Sunday newspaper at the corner café across the road. I conscientiously did so. On returning I carefully handed him the paper and change through the car window. He immediately noticed that I had taken two papers instead of one and asked me to return it – the Sunday papers were usually so thick and cluttered with inserts that I had not realised. I turned around to run across the road surprised by the screeching of brakes. I leapt so high in the air from fright that it seemed like I completely cleared the bonnet of the VW Beetle that nearly ran me over. Sheepishly, I went into the café to return the paper that I hadn't paid for. I can't remember all that Dad and Mom said on returning to the car but to this day I am much more careful when crossing a road. While I am very grateful that God protected me that day from possibly life- changing injuries, the enduring lesson I learnt was that of financial honesty. That's the kind of man Dad was. Although there was only 'small change' involved the principle is huge.

Although Dad was mostly at home when not working, I experienced him as physically and emotionally absent. I can't remember him ever hugging me as a child or expressing his love or affection for me. It was only in my mid-twenties that I discovered that he had always loved me deeply. He was just unable to express it in emotional or physical ways. Raised by a harsh taskmaster of a father, he was taught that 'cowboys don't cry' and not to show emotions to children, especially little boys.

The result was that I projected that experience of a father onto God, The Heavenly Father. I thought of God as detached, distant and uninvolved in my life. In my mind, I had relegated him to ruling the universe from somewhere outside of time and space – somewhere far removed from me.

In my mid-twenties I was preparing some ministry material when a memory flashed into my mind of my father and me having a fight. I had responded disrespectfully to a remark he made about my appearance. I vividly remember the anger on my father's face while he was lashing out at me with his fists, my mother cupping her head in her hands at the kitchen table and me being wedged in-between the wall and the refrigerator while trying to ward of his blows. This incident had happened more than ten years previously and I had forgotten it for most of that time. I was surprised at the clarity of the recollection and simultaneously embarrassed that it had ever happened. God was silent. He didn't say any more but I knew that He had said a lot. I was immediately convicted of dishonouring my dad and knew that I had to put things right with him. It was weeks later that I was able to do so.

It happened to be Father's Day. After giving him a gift and catching up on the family news my father and I went into his bedroom to speak privately. I asked him if he remembered the incident when we had the terrible fight in the kitchen when I was a teenager. I thought he would probably have to scratch his head and think for a while. He didn't. He immediately became emotional and said that he remembered, in fact that he remembered very well. I duly apologized for dishonouring him and being such a bad example of a Christian teenager. He embraced me and willingly expressed forgiveness.

He then held me by the shoulders, looked me in the eyes and asked me to forgive him for lashing out at me that day and not always being the father that I had needed. And then he said something that blew me away. He explained how he had remembered that incident almost every day since it had happened. He felt guilty about it. It was like a sword hanging over his head. All those years he had a longing in his heart to clear the air with me. He just did not know how. Although he had many times determined in his heart to talk to me about it, when it came to the point, he just did not know how to broach the subject. He thanked me profusely for giving him the opportunity to get it off his chest in being able to apologise.

That day I realized for the first time that my dad had always loved me deeply. He just hadn't known how to express it. He longed for relationship and fellowship with me – just like any dad would. From that moment our relationship radically changed and it started having a profound effect on how I related to God as a father. I realized that God also longed for fellowship and relationship with me and not to give Him that opportunity would frustrate His great big Father heart. I also started to recall times when I would wake up at night and my dad would be standing next to my bed. When he saw I was awake he would shuffle out of the room. I don't know if he did that every night or just the few nights that I happened to wake up but I now know that was his way of expressing his love to me.

On my fifty-eighth birthday – the last before my dad graduated to eternity - I was chatting to him on a long-distance phone call. Apart from wishing me happy birthday and reminding me of the events on the day I was born he expressed his appreciation for me and said that he could not remember a day of pain or shame that I had caused him or my mother in the last fifty-eight years. I told him that I thought he had a short memory, even though he was not suffering from dementia! I was deeply touched that in his heart there were no unresolved issues.

That's exactly how God our heavenly Father sees us. When we are reconciled to Him in Christ all distance between Him and us is cancelled and He chooses to forget our sins and failings as if they never existed. We often still try to remind God of our past and how bad we are but He has no recollection of it. He chooses not to remember. He has forgiven us completely, embraced us as His children, and loves us absolutely. That's His Father heart.

A Father's Concern

Fathers generally have a natural in-built concern for the wellbeing of their children. As a result, they are willing to sacrifice for them and go to great lengths to ensure that their children are provided for. My dad did his utmost to provide for the family and make sure we were all well taken care of and that we children could have a good education even at great personal expense to himself. Initially he was very opposed to me giving up a career in civil engineering and becoming a full-time missionary but soon became one of our most ardent and consistent supporters over more than two decades.

As a father, I have a deep concern for the wellbeing of my children and have discovered a readiness in my own life to go without so that my children can have. I don't even see it as a sacrifice but as an immense privilege. No need to feel sorry for me – that's what dads do.

In August 2011 David and I were climbing Kilimanjaro, to celebrate my sixtieth birthday and his graduation. As we approached our final day of the climb to the summit David was ill because of the altitude and lack of oxygen. He had not eaten well for two days owing to loss of appetite and was struggling with nausea and headaches. We started our last 1200 metre climb at midnight under a full moon: no need for headlamps. It was -13oC. It was tough going at the best of times and David was struggling from the onset of acute mountain sickness. I physically pushed him up some of the steeper sections. Our two guides were excellent, often pausing to give us sips of warm tea from a flask. They only allowed us to stop for two to three minutes at a time for fear that our bodies would get the message that we had stopped and start 'shutting down'.

When we reached the top of the crater at Gillman's Point at 5685 metres, only 210 meters from the summit, the guides determined that David had to descend immediately. His life was at risk. He wanted to argue the case for staying slightly longer but we had signed an undertaking that if the guides thought it in our best interest to descend, we would comply immediately. Besides, we had promised Cecilia that we would not take undue risks. David then said that we had agreed that if I needed to turn back, he would accompany me but if he had to turn back I would stay and try to complete the climb. I couldn't remember such an agreement.

We warmly embraced and prayed together. Within five minutes of reaching Gillman's Point, David was being led on the descent by our senior guide who was on his hundredth climb. He knew what he was doing. I stayed on the mountain for another hour and a half. I climbed to Uhuru Peak and visited the glaciers hugging the rim of the volcanic crater. I stretched out my hands and prayed: 'Nkosi sikelele iafrika – God bless Africa!' I tried to savour the moment of being on 'the roof of Africa' but that hour and a half was dominated by my concern for my son. As were the few hours of my descent. It was the most painful part of my whole climb. That made me even more concerned about David. How had he coped! I was relieved back at base camp to be reunited with him. He had survived the initial excruciatingly steep descent of 1000 metres and was doing reasonably okay. We descended another 1000 metres together to overnight where the air was more oxygenated and completed our descent the following day. It took David another ten days or so to fully recover.

Although I was willing to go to great lengths to support him, even at huge risk of me not completing the climb myself, the most agonizing part for me of the whole gruelling expedition was the emotional strain and overwhelming concern for David. It far outweighed the physical exertion. That's what fathers do!

In a similar way God, our heavenly Father, is unquestionably concerned for our wellbeing and constantly wants the best for us. If my dad was willing to sacrifice for my wellbeing and that of my siblings and I am willing to forgo for my children's benefit, and we are only human, how much more is God our heavenly Father willing to sacrifice for our wellbeing? And He has! Jesus sacrificed His life to show us how much God the Father really loves us and values us.

Unconditional Love

In the time and place in which I grew up it was subconsciously understood that love and acceptance were based on performance. The more you wanted to satisfy your basic need for acceptance the more you had to perform and pretend that you were okay.

In 1986 I was on a flight from Los Angeles to Amsterdam. I noticed a couple checking into the seats in front of me and recognised the husband as Dr Richard Wurmbrand. He was in his late seventies and was accompanied by his wife Sabina. I had met him previously at a missions conference in South Africa and remember being shown the torture marks on his body. I had also read his book Tortured for Christ. So, I took the liberty of introducing myself to them. Understandably, he did not recognise me but did remember the conference he had spoken at. To me, Richard Wurmbrand was one of those heroes of the faith, a general in ministry.

He was a Romanian Christian minister of Jewish descent who had been imprisoned and tortured for his views that Christianity and communism were not compatible. He initially spent eight and a half years in prison, three of which were in solitary confinement. He was later sentenced to another twenty-five years for continuing to preach. After five years, he was released during a time of amnesty and ransomed by the Norwegian Mission to the Jews and the Hebrew Christian Alliance for $10,000 (although the going rate for political prisoners was $1,900) and allowed to leave the country.

During the long overnight transatlantic flight, he paced up and down the aisle, obviously unable to sleep. He would stop at my seat for a moment of fellowship. On one occasion he exhorted me to always have a word of encouragement for people. He also encouraged me to strive for excellence in the ministry. He said it was a shame to be a good preacher: you need to be excellent. At another stage he said to me, 'You need to read yourself full, pray yourself hot, and preach yourself empty.' These were precious words that I immediately wrote down in my journal.

On one of his meanderings past my seat he noticed me paging through some leadership material and paused to give me a short lecture on leadership. He then asked me if I was an officer in the Lord's army. I hesitated for a moment to consider whether I was a junior officer or maybe a captain but before I could say anything he challenged me with, 'Young man, don't stoop to be a captain if you can be a general,' and then proceeded to lecture me on the virtues of being ambitious for the Kingdom of God.

I have realised that it is vitally important to be ambitious for the Kingdom of God for myself and equally for others. I have also recognised, more importantly, that my sense of worth and identity is not in what I do but in my relationship with Father God and His unconditional love and acceptance of me.

It was a liberating discovery. I didn't have to do anything to be loved by God and there is nothing I have done that is so terrible that causes Him to love me less. God's love for me is not based on what I have done or not done but on who He is. God does not love me because I have given my life to Him or because I have given money to the poor or because of anything I have done. He loves me because He loves me, because He loves me, because He loves me, because He is love.

You see, you can be sold out to Jesus and be totally submitted to His Lordship. Your life can be displaying the fruit of the Spirit, representing the character of Christ, and people can be drawn to you to eat of that fruit. You can also be moving powerfully in ministry, with the Holy Spirit manifesting His presence in supernatural ways through you with all kinds of miracles. But at the end of the day when you lay your head on the pillow you are just a child – a child of God - and if you don't know Him as your Father, there is something lacking.

I apply myself to work hard and strive for excellence in life and ministry but I find my identity and sense of value in the unconditional love of the Father. I don't have to perform to be loved by God. He already does. I do want to perform, though, to get the job done of doing what God has called me to do on earth. I serve Him with all my strength not because I want Him to love me more but because I have discovered that He already loves me unconditionally. I don't serve God to earn His favour but because I have already tasted His favour.

You do not have to perform to be loved by God. In fact God loved you when you were performing very badly. The Bible teaches us that while we were still sinners Christ died for us. It had nothing to do with our performance or lack of performance but had everything to do with the grace and mercy of a loving God with a massive Father heart. This understanding should embarrass us out of our selfishness and sin and motivate us to live a life pleasing to Him. The least I can do to say thank you to Him for all He has done for me is to dedicate my entire life to Him and live for Him wholeheartedly.

Jesus the Revelation of The Father

For years I had a different perception of God than I had of Jesus. I had this strange notion that Jesus was the merciful expression of God, while God the Father was a militant figure sitting in Heaven with a baseball bat ready to knock me over the head as soon as I stepped out of line. I saw Jesus as forgiving and compassionate and viewed God as a harsh judge – distant and uninvolved. Through being exposed to teaching on the nature and character of God I thankfully realised that that is not true! I discovered that God the Father is as loving and compassionate as Jesus. He is as kind and as gentle and as forgiving as Jesus.

It was a refreshing and life-changing revelation to me that Jesus came to show us what the Father is really like. Jesus came to put Him on display and to introduce Him to us. Jesus came to exemplify the Father.

In John 14:6,7 Jesus says to his disciples, 'I am the way and the truth and the life. No one comes to the Father except through me. If you really know me, you will know my Father as well. From now on, you do know him and have seen him.' Even after this clear statement Philip asks Jesus to reveal the Father to them and Jesus replies, 'Don't you know me, Philip, even after I have been among you such a long time? Anyone who has seen me has seen the Father. How can you say, "Show us the Father"?' (John 14:9).

This understanding radically affected my appreciation for and relationship with God the Father.

The Quantity and Quality of God's Love

The further revelation of scripture that God loves me now as much as He ever will, and also that He loves me as much as He loves Jesus, blew my mind. What an amazing thought!

In South Africa there was a television commercial for a coffee creamer called Cremora. The advertisement depicted a man with his head almost in the refrigerator obviously looking for something. In frustration he calls out, 'Where is the Cremora?' From somewhere in the house you hear the voice of a woman, supposedly that of his wife, shout out, 'It's not inside; it's on top.' The camera then focuses on the large jar of Cremora on top of the refrigerator while the man says with bated breath and deliberate enunciation 'IT'S NOT INSIDE; IT'S ON TOP!'

Often when I have declared to an audience that all I am going to do is tell them that 'God loves them', I get the feeling that they think I am going to waste their time. Why tell them something they already know? Because it is only on top. It is only theory and good theology and not a personal internalised revelation or understanding of the heart.

I too had always believed theoretically and theologically that 'God is Love' (1 John 4:8) and that 'God so loved the world that He sent His son' (John 3:16). But for a long time it was not inside it was only on top! That all changed when I personally encountered the accepting love of God the Father in our preparation as adopters.

In His High Priestly prayer in John seventeen, just before Jesus is betrayed and led away to be crucified, He prays the most serious and important prayer of His life. Jesus is agonising in prayer for his followers and pleads with the Father that 'the world may know that You have sent Me, and have loved them as You have loved Me' (John 17:23 NKJV).

Wow! God loves us as much as He loves Jesus.

How much does God love Jesus? Infinitely, immaculately, impeccably, perfectly, faultlessly and we run out of adverbs to describe it. It is more than - so high you can't get over it, so wide you can't get around it and so deep you can't get under it. It is indeterminable! The amazing thing is that He loves us with the same quality and quantity of love that He loves Jesus!

My first reaction after reading that was: Impossible! God can't love me as much as He loves Jesus. I am not like Jesus! Maybe one day when I am more Christ-like He will love me more. When I am perfect He will love me perfectly. Immediately a spirit of comparison and performance kicked in. I had to perform to earn God's acceptance and favour.

And then the penny dropped. God did not love me as much as he loved Jesus because I was like Jesus, but as if I was. It had nothing to do with me and my performance but had everything to with who He was – a loving Father.

In John 15:9 Jesus also reveals to us that He too loves us as much as the Father loves Him: 'As the Father has loved me, so have I loved you. Now remain in my love'.

In Matthew 22:37-39 Jesus summarises all the Law and the Prophets into the following statement, 'Love the Lord your God with all your heart and with all your soul and with all your mind. This is the first and greatest commandment. And the second is like it: Love your neighbour as yourself'.

It is my opinion that God keeps both these commandments. First, He loves Himself with all His heart, soul, mind and strength. He has no problem with His identity or His self-worth. He is completely secure and comfortable with who He is. And besides that, because He is Love and is willing the highest good for His entire creation and wanting the best for all of us, He needs to find the being in the universe that is the most valuable and promote the good of that being for the good of everybody. He just happens to be that being! So both God and us have to put God first.

Secondly, He loves His neighbour as He loves Himself. Who is His neighbour? Do I hear some people saying, Jesus and The Holy Spirit? Yes, they are but more importantly, you. You are God's neighbour! And if He loves His neighbour as He loves Himself that means He loves you as much as He loves Himself. That is another way of saying Jesus loves you as much as the Father loves Him (John 15:9) and God the Father loves you as much as He loves Jesus (John 17:23). Let that revelation sink from your head to your heart, from on top to inside. Embrace it with all your being.

If I, as a normal human being and an imperfect father, have the ability to love my biological son as much as I love my three adopted children - remember the sequence in which I learnt to love them - then how much more does the perfect heavenly Father have the ability to love and accept us, His adopted children, as much as He loves His own son, Jesus. That's all I have been trying to emphasise in this chapter and that is the basis of the Father heart of God - He loves us as much as He loves Jesus.

Blockages

Like me, you have probably been in a shower where the water just drips instead of gushing over you with vibrancy and pleasant pressure. There is usually one of two problems. Either too many people have showered before you and the supply has run dry or there is nothing wrong with the supply but the pipes are blocked with all kinds of muck and limescale.

When it comes to God's love for us there is nothing wrong with the supply. It is readily available, perfect in quality and unlimited in quantity. If you as a child of God are not experiencing the refreshing love of the Father showering over you daily, then there are blockages somewhere. There is nothing wrong with the supply. It is infinite like a shoreless ocean.

In the next chapter I will share some of the blockages or hindrances to experiencing God's love.

oOo

Chapter 4
Hindrances to God's Love

For I am convinced that neither death nor life,
neither angels nor demons, neither the present
nor the future, nor any powers, neither height
nor depth, nor anything else in all creation,
will be able to separate us from the love of
God that is in Christ Jesus our Lord.
Romans 8:38,39

Though our feelings come and go,
God's love for us does not.
C. S. Lewis

Our Frame of Reference

Imagine a gold-framed portrait of your favourite personality hanging on the wall. One day you decide to redecorate the room and on removing the portrait from its hook you accidently drop it on the floor. The frame smashes and the corners break and are no longer at right angles. The frame is now askew. What happens to the portrait? It is warped and deformed. The picture no longer looks like the original. Many people have a warped or skewed picture of God, not because He is warped but because their frame of reference of who He is has been twisted and bent by their experiences in life.

Cecilia and I were once invited to share some of our life story at a Ladies Tea. Afterwards one of the women came up to me and said that she enjoyed my speech (that said a lot) but that she couldn't relate to the warm emotional way in which we talked about God. I asked her what her view of God was. She pointed towards a skylight in the ceiling and said that she thought of God as a big positive mystical force out there somewhere. I replied that it was no wonder that she couldn't relate to God personally and emotionally and that I couldn't relate to such a god either. I added that I thought of God as a person with all the elements of personality. He has emotions, is highly intelligent and can think, reason and remember. He even chooses to forget. She found that interesting and at least wanted to go away and think about it.

Our 'frame of reference' or concept of God the Father is directly influenced by our relationship with our earthly fathers; our experiences with authority figures in our lives; our concept of the will of God; the traumatic experiences that we had; and our self-worth or self-love (or lack of it).

Earthly Fathers

In the previous chapter I explained the effect that my relationship with my earthly father had on my perception of my heavenly Father and how God in His grace redeemed that.

Over more than four decades I have ministered to people, especially young people, who have grown up without a father or with an abusive, absent or irresponsible father. We have witnessed the refreshing, restoring and healing power of God's love as they have experienced the acceptance and embrace of God, the Father.

Early on in our ministry I was praying with a young man in his mid-twenties who was struggling to trust God. I remembered from previous times together that he had lost his father when he was young, but I couldn't remember the details so I asked him to refresh my memory. He recalled being a little four-year-old boy, sitting alone in a room and weeping. Someone had just told him that his dad had gone to be with Jesus and that he would not be coming home that day. He presumed it was his mother that broke the news to him although he could not definitely recall that detail. What he did realise, however, was that he wasn't crying out of grief for his dad's death – as a little boy he hadn't understood all those implications yet - but that he was crying out of disappointment because his dad was not going to return home that afternoon to take him on a train journey to the next town, as he had promised. He concluded that the tears he was crying then were tears of disappointment rather than grief.

As he was relating this memory the Holy Spirit reminded me that not only is God an omnipresent Father but also a Father of the fatherless (Psalm 68:5). In my mind's eye I could see the room full of God's presence and the Father kneeling next to him and comforting him. I prayed as the Holy Spirit led me, that this dimension of God's loving presence would be added to that hurtful memory, and witnessed how the young man experienced the healing power of God the Father's love. The long-held disappointment of not being taken on the train ride was dealt with and he could now start growing in his ability to trust God. He realised that he had been reluctant to trust God and take risks out of fear of being disappointed again.

We see in the New Testament Jesus going out of His way to reconstruct a situation to add His reconciling, restoring, forgiving, healing, and loving presence into the most disappointing moment in Peter's life. In the eighteenth chapter of the gospel of John it refers to

Peter huddled up to a 'fire of coals' warming himself. He had already been asked once if he knew Jesus, which he denied. It was around the fire where he denied that he knew Jesus the second and third time. The cock crowed to signal the dawning of a new day – the darkest in Peter's life. His life had hit rock bottom. He had turned his back on Jesus when his master needed him the most. This most disappointing moment would have been permanently etched in his psyche.

A few days later, after Jesus' resurrection from the dead, we read in John chapter twenty-one how Jesus goes out of His way before dawn to construct a 'fire of coals' with fish and bread cooking on it. As the disciples warm themselves around the fire and enjoy the intimate fellowship of a meal with Jesus, He focuses on Peter and asks him three times 'Do you love me?' Peter affirms three times that he loves Jesus. Jesus re-commissions him to 'Go and feed my sheep'. A new day had dawned for Peter. The deep disappointment of the denial and the indelibly imprinted sound of the cock crowing at the crack of dawn had been replaced by the accepting, forgiving presence of Jesus and His gentle voice. A bright future lay ahead.

Cecilia and I were once praying for a lady while sitting on either side of her. I had laid my hand on her shoulder and was praying that she would experience the hand of God touching her life in an equally real and tangible way. At one stage I prayed that she would be able to sit on the Father's lap as His child and experience His love and acceptance. She interrupted my prayer and asked me not to pray like that. I realised that I had offended her somehow. She started weeping and said that she couldn't relate to sitting on God the Father's lap. Many times, when she had sat on her father's lap as a child he would treat her disrespectfully. That memory came flooding back to her and it was obviously deeply painful. Her experience of her earthly father had become a major hindrance to experiencing intimacy with God and the love that He as a Father had for her.

We have seen dozens - if not hundreds - of people deeply transformed by discovering the love of God the Father as their source of value and worth, rather than that of their earthly father. For some, the revelation has been dramatic and the change quick. For others, the healing has been a process and the journey a little longer. The effect of finding their place in the heart of God their Father and discovering their identity as His child has been equally profound.

Authority Figures

A colleague and I were ministering to a gentleman in his mid-seventies after a talk on the Love of God. He told us that he had given his life to Jesus when he was young and that he was a Christian out of sheer determination because he believed that it was the right way to live. He served God out of religious conviction but there was no emotion or relationship involved. He wasn't relating to our message on the warm embracing and accepting love of God the Father. As he was telling us this, my friend had a 'word of knowledge' that the man had been deeply wounded when he was twelve years old. Initially the man could not remember anything in particular, but after a while a hurtful memory flooded into his mind. He recounted an incident as a twelve-year-old boy being ridiculed and denounced by a teacher in the front of the classroom and before all his classmates. He couldn't recall what triggered the incident but remembered in detail how the teacher crushed a stick of chalk and rubbed it into his hair, then slapped him all over his upper body with a chalk-filled duster while mocking him.

He was then asked to stand in the corner of the room for the rest of the class feeling totally humiliated and alone.

We started praying for the healing power of God's love and acceptance to be added to that hurtful memory. We believe that Jesus was standing with him in that corner and had carried all that scorn and shame upon the cross for him. As we prayed the dimension of Jesus was added to that memory. He could embrace the grace of God, release forgiveness towards the teacher and be healed from the pain and shame of that moment. He testified that at the age of seventy-five he now knew for the first time, from his heart, that he had a loving Father that he could trust.

He later recalled how from that young age he had struggled with authority figures and found it difficult to trust God. He was afraid to commit in case he would be humiliated, let down or disappointed again.

During our more than ten years of local church ministry in the United Kingdom we, sadly, encountered many young adults who had been deeply wounded by over-controlling, legalistic and authoritarian spiritual leaders. It had a profoundly negative effect on their relationship with God and view of church leadership. For some, it took years to be reintegrated into a church community where they felt safe and at home and could make a viable contribution again.

I have found that many people who have been hurt or let down by authority figures, whether they be teachers, coaches, civic or spiritual leaders, subconsciously project that hurt on to God. Because God is absolute authority they just think of Him as a bigger version of the abusive authorities in their lives. It has also been my experience that many have been restored to a trusting relationship with God the Father after this distortion has been rectified by the grace of God.

The 'Will of God'

Because we believe that God is almighty, sovereign, timeless, and all-knowing many would subsequently believe that everything that happens in the world must be His will. That is simply not true! His will is not being done on earth. That's why we are instructed to pray 'your kingdom come, your will be done on earth as it is in heaven' (Matthew 6:10).

On the afternoon of Tuesday 11 September 2001, I walked into our home in a leafy suburb of Pretoria, South Africa. My son Donovan called me to the television as an aircraft had just crashed into a building in New York. Being a private pilot I imagined a light aircraft straying off course and colliding with a skyscraper. As I got to the television I saw the gaping hole in one of the Twin Towers and watched in horror as CNN reported on Flight 175 flying into the Southern Tower just after 9 am (New York time) and then the subsequent collapse of the two iconic buildings, in a cloud of dust. I was glued to the television for hours as a major terrorist attack on New York and the Pentagon was unfolding before my eyes. Almost 3000 lives were lost as a consequence. I was part of a global audience of millions that has that event indelibly imprinted on our soul. 9/11 has now become synonymous with 'the Twin Tower bombings' and the evil of terrorism that blights our world.

On Thursday 7 July 2005, the day after London was proclaimed as the host city for the 2012 Olympic Games, the city was rocked by a major terrorist attack on the London underground. Fifty-two civilians were killed and over 700 people injured, some of them brutally maimed by the atrocious actions of four suicide bombers. I was due to meet with three of my team members at 9 am at the Church office in Regents Park. By 7 am we had called the meeting off because one of them had taken ill and another couldn't make it. I decided to travel to the city anyway after 9:30 am (cheaper fares) to take care of other business. By 9 am the news broke that three bombs had been detonated on the underground tube line and another on a bus. If the four of us had travelled as initially planned that day it is very likely that we would have been on one of the trains bombed or at least caught up in the aftermath and chaos of all the public transport being put in disarray.

These events in New York and London are only two examples of many evil things that happen almost daily in a world that seems to have gone berserk. The question is often, why? Where is God in all this mess? Why does God allow this to happen? Because of our view of God, we often erroneously believe that somehow it is all His will. He must be the one orchestrating this chaos. He is ultimately to blame. That is simply not true!

This might sound like an over-simplification, but let me say it as categorically and as strongly as I know how. God's will is not being done on earth. If you believe that the evil and suffering happening around you is God's will then your view of God is one of an awful angry tyrant. God is not like that!

God never created sin. The devil is the author and creator of all that is evil. God's power is not arbitrary. It is always directed by His love, and so will always accomplish good. If God is sovereign and almighty, why does He allow evil then? He does not allow evil in that He plans it or causes it to happen. He 'allows evil' in that He gives people the right to be wrong. He created us with the ability to choose for Him or against Him, to choose between good and evil. Unfortunately, evil people chose evil deeds and sow havoc on earth affecting many, including the totally innocent. God takes no pleasure in any evil deed or the horrendous consequences on either the entirely guilty or the completely innocent. His heart is broken over the state of His creation.

Why does God not just stop it then, you may ask? He could, but then He would have to suspend the fact that we are created with the unique ability to choose between right and wrong. He would have to stop every evil intention in every person in the whole world to be consistent. And one day He will stop it! But when He does it will be the end of the world.

In his book Mere Christianity C. S. Lewis explains it this way: 'God will invade. But I wonder whether people who ask God to interfere openly and directly in our world quite realise what it will be like when He does. When that happens, it is the end of the world. When the author walks on to the stage the play is over' (p65).

Our creator will step back on to the stage and then, and only then, will all this evil be dealt with. In fact, it will be the end of the world as we know it. In the meantime, we are living in a broken world that was never originally designed that way by God.

Do not lay blame at God's door for anything that He is not to blame for. If I tell you that God loves you with the same quantity and quality of love that He loves Jesus but you directly or indirectly blame God for all the pain and suffering in the world, and more particularly in your life, then it is no wonder that you cannot embrace or experience His great love for you. It is a major hindrance.

Traumatic Experiences

Almost everyone has had some kind of trauma or multiple traumas in their life. Cecilia and I have had our fair share.

We were the first on the scene of a horrendous head-on collision between two cars in the black of night. Seeing lifeless bodies trapped in mangled vehicles and trying to help the wounded while flagging down traffic to avoid further collisions, remains a haunting memory.

At another time I was investigating a power failure in the electricity supply sub-station on our YWAM base when I came across the charred body of an electrocuted cable thief sitting, with hacksaw in his hand, over a ten-centimetre-thick high voltage cable that he had tried to cut through. Traumatic!

The most sobering and harrowing day of my life to date was being taken on a tour of some of the 1994 genocide sites in Rwanda. Over a period of one hundred days between 500,000 and a million Tutsis and Hutus had murdered one another in a bloody tribal war. That day I saw at least 10,000 human skulls piled up in heaps. I also witnessed the aftermath of a massacre that had taken place in a church compound where people had sought refuge. How does this happen? The greatest tragedy of this event is that more than ninety percent of both the Hutu and Tutsi tribes professed to be Christian. Yet they killed one another indiscriminately. They had no concept of integrating godly, biblical principles into their political or tribal agendas.

The year 2011 was traumatic in our household because Cecilia was fighting cancer. She was diagnosed with an aggressive breast cancer and had to undergo three sets of surgery culminating in a full mastectomy followed by months of chemotherapy and then weeks of radiotherapy. When she was asked 'Why you? You have given your life in God's service for the sake of others. Why does God allow such suffering?' Her answer was always a resilient 'Why not me? What makes me so special? I am not going to live forever. We live in a broken world.'

Although traumatic, we experienced the incredible enabling grace of God and the loving support of family and friends throughout this time.

In November 2014 Cecilia and I had a short-lived traumatic experience. We arrived in Pretoria on a Tuesday afternoon from London for a three-week family holiday, which would include four days in Dubai with dear friends on our return. On Wednesday Cecilia complained of stiff ankles and tingling in her hands and toes. We attributed it to the long-haul flight, jet lag and dehydration. On Thursday morning Cecilia woke up with no feeling in her lower legs and hands and could not walk around unaided. By Friday a neurologist had diagnosed her with AIDP (Acute Inflammatory Demyelinating Polyneuropathy also known as Guillain Barre Syndrome) needing immediate hospitalisation and treatment. By that Friday evening we were on a flight back to London.

Initially I felt aggrieved at what was happening. Our long- anticipated holiday was being stolen from us. We were not going to spend time with family and friends and enjoy a much-needed rest. I had learnt in situations like this to lean heavily into God and to trust Him. He quickly reminded me that He was the 'Lord of the harvest' and not me. All that I had control over was the seed in my hand, which included my attitudes. I quickly got my attitude into alignment and submission to His sovereignty. I did not resign myself to the situation fatalistically, but did defer to His Lordship in an attitude of relinquishment and trust.

On the Saturday morning, Cecilia was admitted and treated with IVIG (intravenous immunoglobulin) for Guillain Barre Syndrome under the auspices of the National Neurological Hospital in London. She was discharged after a week with the progress of the demyelination arrested and the condition limited to her lower legs and hands. Within a few weeks she had regained all the feeling in her legs, feet and hands and could function normally again. The more we speak to medical professionals the more we understand what an incredible miracle this is. While we are extremely grateful for medical science, the current technological developments in diagnosis, and the excellent professional care that Cecilia had, we honour God for His miraculous intervention and healing.

We have spoken to, and ministered to, many people who have had traumas of one kind or another much, much worse than that. Some have had their lives radically altered in a painful moment whereas others have had long drawn out traumatic experiences.

I think of a couple caught up in an attempted hijacking, the husband being shot three times though the lower back and groin and being left impotent. God subsequently blessed them with a beautiful daughter.

I think of a young lady that experienced a generation of sexual abuse from her father. She has been redeemed from the shame, subsequent depression and bitterness, and is released into a redemptive ministry to others.

I think of a Rwandan colleague I ministered alongside in the inner city of Pretoria in 2002. Both he and his wife were deeply traumatised by the genocide (he a Tutsi and she a Hutu). They tried to escape the atrocities by taking refuge in a mission compound that subsequently came under attack from vigilantes. He was shot through his leg and his wife feigned death as she lay under a heap of corpses. They got separated in the aftermath – each thinking that the other had been killed.

He recounted his agonising recovery and tormenting long walk to a refugee camp in Tanzania. He shared how demeaned he felt when he discovered he was more excited to encounter wild animals or corpses along the way rather than people who were alive, as he didn't know whom he could trust any longer. He and his wife were reconnected by 'coincidence' two years later when he left his refugee camp to travel to another to minister the gospel. They have largely recovered from the trauma by the amazing grace of God, have a beautiful family of four children, and are now serving the purposes of God in the United States of America.

It has been my experience that if these traumatic experiences, that are completely out of our control, are not dealt with by the grace of God they become breeding grounds for contempt and resentment towards Him. At the very least they are major blockages to our intimacy with God and access to His infinitely refreshing Father's love for us.

In 2009 my dad was diagnosed with severe liver cancer and sent home from hospital. Within a day he went into a semi-coma and within three days he passed away. As I prepared for his funeral and contemplated what he must have gone through during those three days, I imagined him all alone in a dark tunnel. I was reminded of the scripture 'The people remained at a distance, while Moses approached the thick darkness where God was' (Exodus 20:21) and took comfort from the fact that God the Father is with us even during the deepest darkness we might find ourselves in.

Selflove

I am convinced that we are supposed to love ourselves. There are no less than seven passages in scripture where we are instructed to 'love our neighbour as we love ourselves'. Nowhere are we challenged to love our neighbour without the qualification 'as ourselves'. The Bible presupposes that we have a healthy self-love. You may love yourself. Not only may you, you must.

God is love and He is the source of all love including the love we are to have for ourselves. Maybe you find it difficult to believe that God loves you as much as He loves Jesus. At least believe that He loves you a lot more than you thought. Allow the unconditional love and acceptance of the Father to nourish your soul and restore your sense of value and worth. Don't allow a lack of self-love to become a hindrance to the release of the abundant love of God in your life.

The dilemma is, if you don't love yourself you won't be able to give or receive love. If someone tells you that God loves you or that they love you and you don't think much of yourself then it is impossible for you to receive that love. You don't believe that God, or anybody else for that matter, really loves you if you don't even love yourself.

If you don't love and accept yourself, you can't receive love from God and others. If you don't receive love you have no love to give either. It becomes a vicious circle. It is comparable to the petals of a flower closed like a clenched fist. How do we break free of this cycle? By receiving a revelation of God's love for us. I am a staunch believer that the unconditional accepting love of God the Father for us is the most powerful, restorative healing force in the universe.

It can be as simple as thanking God that He loves us and accepts us and asking Him to pour His unconditional love into our hearts. When we allow even a little sliver of God's love to refresh our soul it is like releasing one finger of that closed fist. As we taste His love and acceptance we start feeling a bit better about ourselves. We then start to open up a bit more to receive and give love to others. As we do that, more of God's love is poured into our hearts. That enables us to love ourselves more and to love others, in turn. As the cycle continues we blossom like a beautiful flower in the radiant sunshine of His love – and become the person He has created us to be.

I historically equated self-love to selfishness and thought of self-love as sinful and self-hatred as virtuous until I grasped the fact that Jesus fully embraced His identity and loved Himself in a healthy way without one speck of selfishness or sin in it. The great biblical chapter on love, 1 Corinthians thirteen, teaches that 'love is not self-seeking or selfish' (13:5 CEV). God intends for us to love ourselves in a healthy way without being selfish about it. In fact, I sincerely believe that a healthy self-acceptance based in self-love is the key, both to living unselfishly and to denying ourselves on behalf of God and others.

Jesus is the example of all three of these things. He had no problem with His self-worth or identity. He accepted and loved Himself. He lived for the glory of God and the sake of others. He was a servant leader and totally unselfish. He denied Himself and gave His life as a ransom for the salvation of all mankind. Jesus shows us what it looks like to live unselfishly, denying ourselves, and yet loving ourselves.

When I officiate at a wedding ceremony, at a certain point in the proceedings I ask the bride and then the guests what they think her greatest need might be. I then suggest that her greatest need is that the man she is about to marry loves himself, because if he doesn't she is in trouble. If he doesn't love himself where must the love come from with which he is supposed to love her? And similarly, if she doesn't love herself where will her love come for her husband. I then go on to explain that God is the source of all love. Only once we have discovered the depth of His love for us, can we feel comfortable with ourselves and then share that love deeply with others. Marriage requires a high degree of self-denial and unselfishness. The key to both is a healthy self-love based in the security of God's abundant love and acceptance of us.

There are probably many other hindrances to us experiencing the fullness of God the Father's intimate love for us but we can take courage in the fact that the Bible reassures us that nothing can separate us from the love of God in Christ Jesus (Romans 8:38,39).

oOo

Chapter 5
Being Real

In Him was life, and that life was the light of all mankind.
The light shines in the darkness, and the
darkness has not overcome it.
John 1:4,5

We must be the same person in private and in public.
Only the Christian worldview gives us
the basis for this kind of integrity.
Chuck Colson

The quest of my life is to be real. To discover a freedom on the one hand to be myself and to live out my unique design, while on the other hand walking in wholeness and integrity. I have an insatiable desire to be free from the trappings of tradition and legalism, from inferiority and the fear of man, and to discover simple principles to live by.

One of the first things that God did for me as a young man was to set me free from myself. Most of my years as a teenager and young adult were governed by an overdeveloped concern for what people thought of me. I had a spirit of comparison and a striving to be like others.

I have memories of my mathematics teacher in high school, Mr Taylor, singling me out to do algebraic equations on the chalkboard in front of the whole class. While I was reasonably confident in doing the maths the journey from the back of the classroom to the front seemed ever so far. I was concerned about what my classmates thought of me, conscious of how I was dressed, aware that my hair might be untidy, and worried about my handwriting on the board. If anyone in the class giggled I just knew that they were laughing at me. I was in bondage to their opinions and not free to be myself. A desire developed in me to be free from all that junk and to just be me.

While I 'gave my life to Jesus' when I was ten years old, my recollection of the first ten years or so of my Christian walk and attending church regularly is one of outward conformity to legalistic expectations and religious form. Apart from learning Bible stories in Sunday School and being confronted with the moral lessons they implied, I can't recall ever being challenged on character issues or being discipled in any intentional way. It all seemed very superficial, plastic, and artificial. I longed for a real deep intimate relationship with God.

In 1974, while attending the School of Evangelism in Lausanne, Cecilia and I were sitting in our room one afternoon looking out over the Swiss Alps and the shimmering Lake Geneva in the distance. We were discussing the nudge we both felt in our hearts that maybe our gap year wasn't going to be so short after all. We were wondering if perhaps God wanted us to consider being involved in full-time ministry.

I expressed to Cecilia that it was okay for her to be called into ministry as she could sing, play the piano and the organ (and the accordion for that matter). I on the other hand couldn't even speak in public with any degree of confidence let alone do any of that. I believed that God could not use me.

Our teacher that week was Jean Darnell. She was from the USA and had been instrumental in the 'charismatic renewal' in the United Kingdom. She had been teaching us on the person of the Holy Spirit. She taught on the 'fruit of the Spirit' as exemplified in the character of

Christ and the presence of God being manifest through what we often refer to as the 'gifts of the Holy Spirit'. That evening she called different categories of people forward for prayer and a prophetic word. At one stage, she was ministering to all the young married couples. There were at least six such couples in the class.

When our turn came, she asked us our names, laid her hands on us and prayed 'in the Spirit' for a while. She then spoke over Cecilia that she would have a ministry of hospitality and that she would always have food on her table and a roof over her head. The second word she had for Cecilia was fulfilled about fifteen years later with the birth of David our fourth child (but that's another story). She then turned to me and said, 'Don you are saying: God you can't use me.' My ears pricked up. God had my attention. The fact that she knew such intimate information about me was supernatural. I listened intently.

She continued to encourage me not to compare myself with other people or strive to be like them but to just be myself. She concluded with the remark 'God has a ministry uniquely just for you.'

I was deeply touched and encouraged and took a major step forward on the journey to freedom from a spirit of comparison and striving. With all respect to the men of God whom I was attempting to be like and trying to emulate, I understood that they could not do what God had called me to do and that God did not expect me to do what he has called them to do. God had a ministry uniquely just for me. Wow!

I also remembered that one of the sentiments I had expressed often during moments of worship since my conversion at the age of ten, one of the deepest sighs of my soul, was 'Oh, to be used of God.' That journey had now begun.

Exposing Legalism and Liberalism

One of the other things that God had to set me free from was legalism – the outward conformity to rules and regulations - rather than an intimate relationship with Him based on love and acceptance. A lot of my initial formation as a Christian had to do with dos and do nots governing superficial behaviour and appearance rather than moral issues of the heart.

As a young adult I realised there was a massive imbalance in my view of truth. Relative truths to do with outward conformity and behaviour had taken centre stage at the expense of absolute truths that had eternal value. I thankfully discovered the difference between legalism and liberalism.

Legalism is taking a relative truth or principle and making it an absolute truth. It is an excessive adherence to formula and laws as an outward religious expression rather than to a personal conviction of faith.

Taking a truth relative to the culture or custom in biblical times and making it an absolute for salvation in our day and age is legalistic. The Ten Commandments as given to Moses by God and passed on to us evolved into hundreds of relative laws and interpretations which if applied religiously and legalistically per the 'letter' of the law rather than the 'spirit' of the law, leads to great bondage and a false sense of spirituality.

In the church tradition that I was raised in, for example, women had to wear head coverings to church supposedly as an indication of their submission to and respect for their father's or husband's authority.

Women were also forbidden to wear 'men's clothes' which meant they were not allowed to wear trousers but could otherwise wear mini-skirts and dress seductively. There were many other customary dos and don'ts that had nothing to do with a loving relationship with a trustworthy God. It didn't make sense to me!

In biblical times the Apostle Paul instructed men to greet one another with a 'holy kiss'. It was relevant in the culture then but not appropriate in our day and age. Jesus instructed his disciples to wash one another's feet as a sign of their humility and solidarity with one another. It was the custom of the day. Today we demonstrate our servanthood and humility in other ways.

Liberalism, on the other hand, is taking an absolute truth and making it a relative truth. Liberalism, says that Jesus is not the only way to God but one of the many ways to God. It acknowledges the historicity of Jesus - the fact that He really existed as a man - but denies that He was God incarnate. Liberals go out of their way to bring the authenticity of the Bible and many absolute moral values into question under the guise of being enlightened. This resulting relativism focusses on the autonomy of man rather than the sovereignty of God. When humankind rather than God calls the shots, and determines what is good and evil, true and false, we are in trouble.

Once a society embraces a truth as relative rather than absolute the goal posts keep shifting and the playing field keeps getting broader and broader. For example, when I was a child all sex outside of marriage was deemed wrong and the sanctity of marriage was upheld. During my teenage years in the 1960s we had the hippie movement with 'free love' and promiscuity promoted through the entertainment media of the day. By the time of writing these memoirs, sexual activity outside of marriage is commonly accepted and the liberal agenda has progressed so far that many countries have adopted same-sex marriage as normal and there are moves afoot for children to choose their own sexual identity when they are in junior school. Soon other sexual deviations, now deemed off-limits, will be condoned as normal behaviour for those who have such preferences.

A lifetime challenge for me is to find the radical middle between legalism on the one hand and liberalism on the other. To find true freedom based in integrity rather than the freedom or liberty espoused by the liberals of the day. To discover truth for myself. The challenge is not to be indifferent, complacent or to conform to the trends of the day. Not to compromise on my own convictions just to be religious on the one hand or politically correct on the other.

Understanding Freedom

Freedom is not the ability to do your own thing. That is licence, which leads to bondage and is not freedom at all. Freedom is not the ability to go to a nightclub on a Friday night and shoot your veins full of drugs or get drunk out of your skull. That is irresponsible and stupid and only leads to a loss of freedom.

True freedom is the ability to do that which you know is right. To live the way God has designed and created you to live.

All of us know enough of what is right – it is engrained in our conscience - but we are not always free to do what we know is right. For example, we know that when we have sinned the right thing to do is repent and embrace the forgiveness of Christ but we are not always quick to take responsibility and to do so. Something is holding us back, probably pride. We are not free to do the right thing.

When we have wronged someone, we know that the right thing to do is apologise to him or her and put it right, yet we are seldom quick to do so. In fact, we sometimes wait a long time. Something is holding us back, probably fear – a concern for what they might think of us. We are in bondage to the 'fear of man' and not free to do the right thing.

Financially we know that it is right to be generous and to honour God with the first fruit of our income but we often think the we cannot afford to do so. Something is holding us back. It could be greed or a fear of the future. We are not free to trust God and do the right thing.

We are challenged and encouraged by Jesus with the following: 'If you hold to my teaching, you are really my disciples. Then you will know the truth, and the truth will set you free' (John 8:31,32).

Being Authentic.

Authenticity is the quality of being genuine or legitimate. Being authentic is being true to our original design – to the way we were created. Our original blueprint is Christ. God's intended purpose and design for us is to be Christ-like.

The following scripture gives us a hint of our destiny: 'For those God foreknew he also predestined to be conformed to the image of his Son, that he might be the firstborn among many brothers and sisters' (Romans 8:29). In other words God determined ahead of time that He wanted us to be like Jesus. Or as this paraphrase puts it, 'God knew what he was doing from the very beginning. He decided from the outset to shape the lives of those who love him along the same lines as the life of his Son. The Son stands first in the line of humanity he restored. We see the original and intended shape of our lives there in Him' (Romans 8:29 MSG).

The Greek word used for 'first-born' is the same as for prototype. Jesus is the original, the prototype of all those to follow. God's pre-determined destiny for us is to be conformed to the original as revealed in His son.

If you were to order a new car or the latest electronic gadget based on the prototype, you could make some cosmetic changes as to a preferred colour and changes to outward trimmings, but you cannot change the essence of the design or DNA, if you will. You and I may have different shells and cosmetic trimmings but we are all to conform to the original DNA of our design – that of Christ.

Jesus did not only come to be an example for us but also as an example of us. He came to vindicate God's original design of mankind created in His image. He came to show us that someone in a human form, created in the image and likeness of God, could live in a holy, obedient relationship with Him without the need to sin.

Being Real – Jesus the Example of Us

In Him was life, and that life was the light of all mankind. The light shines in the darkness, and the darkness has not overcome it (John 1:4,5).

The following schematic diagram of this verse has helped me understand the concept of Being Real.

Life – JESUS – Light
Darkness

The 'Him' referred to in John 1:4 is Jesus who from the beginning was God and created all things. He is central to all that is authentic and real.

First, He is the source of life. By implication there is no real life outside of Jesus Christ, only existence. I quickly realised that whatever I was doing outside of Christ wasn't real but was merely artificial or pretence. I could be fit and healthy and accomplish much in my own strength but if I wasn't in Him, I was merely existing and not truly living. Jesus promised that He came to give us life and life in much more abundance. That is the life I crave: an adventurous, exciting, exuberant, effervescent, 'living it up' kind of life. I want to live LIFE – in blazing capitals - to the fullest.

Secondly, I realised that His life was the source of light. My life produced no light. All my human effort and pretence only added to the darkness if it was from behind a facade. If I wanted to produce light and be light in a dark world I needed to live where Christ lived, in the light. I needed to live His life, His attitude, His character, His servanthood, His humility. His life was the light of the world. Not mine.

Thirdly, everything above the line in the diagram is where reality and authenticity happens. Anything that happens from behind a mask or in the realm of darkness and is then presented or projected into the realm of the light, is by implication pretence, artificial and unreal.

As I contemplated the implications of living in the realm of reality where Jesus lives, I was confronted by the need to build the following three characteristics into my life as a matter of priority. They have been an abiding, almost daily pursuit for most of my life. They are confidence that comes from a clear conscience; humility that exemplifies the attitude of Christ; openness that implies walking in the light.

The next few chapters will be taken up with my journey in this regard.

oOo

Chapter 6
Confidence and the Fear of God

So I strive always to keep my conscience
clear before God and man.
Acts 24:16

We were created for clear conscience living. Sin, guilt and shame were never part of our original design.

Confidence from a Clear Conscience.

I have learnt to put a high premium on a clear conscience. To value or prioritise what the Bible calls a 'conscience void of offence toward God and toward man' (Acts 24:16 KJV). Next to my relationship with God, I regard it as my most valuable possession. To lay my head down at night and know there are no unresolved issues between me and God and between me and any other person is extremely liberating and a great way to live.

I am not naturally very confident. In fact, I grew up a little shy and reserved. Having the personality profile of an introvert means that I was not usually the life of a party or the focus of attention. I have discovered, however, that to live in the realm of reality rather than superficially or with pretence, requires a qualified confidence and not just a confident personality. This confidence needs to emanate from my character and be based in a clear conscience.

The following two verses have become some of the foundational scriptures in my life: 'Beloved, if our heart does not accuse us, we have confidence toward God. And whatever we ask, we receive from Him, because we keep His commandments and do those things that are pleasing in His sight' (1 John 3:21,22 NKJV).

I am not at all legalistic about my devotions or so-called 'quiet time'. The effectiveness of my day is not dependant on having a quiet time at the start of the day but on my relationship with God. In order to build and maintain my relationship with God I do have a regular rhythm of prayer and Bible reading. It is part of that regular devotional routine to pray the following prayer often: 'Search me, O God, and know my heart: try me, and know my thoughts: And see if there be any wicked way in me, and lead me in the way everlasting' (Psalm 139:23,24 KJV).

Initially I was reluctant to pray this prayer because every time I did the Holy Spirit would highlight an issue that I needed to put right. But I quickly realised that when the Holy Spirit does bring conviction, it is always very loving, kind, merciful, gentle and specific. I recognised that the Holy Spirit was for me and not against me. He was there to guide me and help me. It has become an abiding principle in my life to welcome the conviction of the Holy Spirit and to respond accordingly.

It is not my practice to be introspective and to go digging for stuff that may or may not be in my heart. I open my heart and invite the Holy Spirit to do that. He does a much more precise and loving job and, besides, I could easily deceive myself.

The most extreme introvert can have loads of confidence if it is based in a clear conscience and emanates from a sound character. Extroverts can mistakenly rely on their outgoing personality to hide the lack of real confidence based in their character. So, let me reiterate before moving on – the confidence that I am talking about is qualified in a clear conscience. It emanates from our character and not our personality.

Two of the biblical principles that have best served my quest for confidence from a clear conscience have been an understanding of the fear of God on the one hand and the paramount importance of forgiveness on the other.

Understanding the Fear of God

As a child and a new Christian, I often heard the 'fear of God' being referred to and that we needed to 'walk in the fear of God' but no one clarified what that meant. I presumed that it had something to do with being frightened or scared of God. The same people that told me to fear God also told me that He loved me and that I needed to love Him with all my heart. It didn't compute for me. Why should I be frightened of someone that loves me and that I endeavored to love with all my being?

Besides, I was convinced that the devil was fearful of God in that he was afraid of God. After all, Jesus had defeated him through His death on the cross and subsequent resurrection. I wanted to be different from the devil. If he was fearful and scared of God, why should I also be fearful and scared of God?

It became abundantly clear to me, of course, that the 'fear of God' had nothing to do with being scared, terrified or fearful of God.

Reverential Respect

The first thing I discovered about the fear of the Lord is that it has to do with an attitude of heart – one of adoration and respect for God. There are several biblical passages that link the fear of God with standing in awe of Him, having reverence for Him as well as praising and worshiping Him: 'Let all the earth fear the LORD; let all the people of the world revere Him' (Psalm 33:8).

In her book Intimate Friendship with God, Joy Dawson writes 'The fear of The Lord should produce in us the same attitude towards sin that God has, which is to hate it. It should also give us a deep respect for and an understanding of the holiness of God' (p21).

The Beginning of Wisdom

Secondly, I understood that the fear of the Lord is linked to wisdom. The Bible not only teaches that it is wise to fear the Lord in the sense that it is good and wise to honour and respect God, but it is also clear from Psalm 111:10 and Proverbs 9:10 that the fear of the Lord is the cornerstone or beginning of wisdom. Without this reverent acknowledgement of God and His holiness you don't even have the beginnings of wisdom, let alone wisdom itself.

I believe that the reason why the political and economic leaders of the world can't solve the complex political and economic problems of the world is because they have no wisdom. And they will be devoid of wisdom until they acknowledge God and give Him the respect and reverence that He is due. The Bible is clear that we should pray for our leaders and those in authority. I have always wondered what to pray and have resolved to at least pray for them to have a good dose of humility and to develop a reverential respect for God; in other words to fear God.

Hating Sin

The third aspect of the fear of the Lord that I came to understand is the most relevant to the context of having confidence from a clear conscience. It has to do with my attitude towards sin. I discovered scriptures that referred to the fear of the Lord as departing from evil, avoiding evil and hating sin.

The simple definition that the fear of the Lord is to hate sin, and by implication is to have a respect for the holiness of God, has had a profound impact on my life. Why? Because you don't willingly and willfully do the things that you hate. If you hate it, you don't do it. If you hate it, you don't do it unless you are forced to. When it comes to sin no one forces us to sin. We sin because we want to, because we like it, because we are not disgusted by it, because we don't hate it.

It is true that we are influenced by our unredeemed nature and the temptations around us, but the bottom line is we sin because we want to, because we like it. When our nature is changed by redemption in Christ we have an added incentive to shun evil. There is an inherent repulsion to sin that comes from honouring and respecting a Holy God and being in a loving relationship with Him.

Think of a foodstuff that you dislike eating or a specific meal you don't particularly enjoy. I can guarantee you that you don't go out of your way every day to find that particular food or prepare that specific meal. Why not? Because you don't like it.

As I was growing up my pet dislike was for green vegetables such as spinach, cabbage and Brussels sprouts. My dad had a penchant for wild spinach called marogo that he used to cultivate in our garden and eat almost every day. I have jokingly said that the only time I got that kind of stuff into my system was when my mother forced it down my throat – she was never really that kind of person. I never willingly ate that stuff! In my sixty-six years on earth I can honestly say that I have not stolen a cabbage plant, a spinach leaf, a handful of marogo or even one Brussels sprout from anybody. In fact, I was never even tempted to do so. I wish I could say that about all sin in my life.

I remember going through a season in my teenage years when I would vacillate between acknowledging that something was sinful on the one hand and justifying that it was not on the other. One Sunday night our pastor read Galatians 6:7 as part of the scripture reading before his sermon: 'Do not be deceived: God cannot be mocked. A man reaps what he sows'.

While I have no recollection of the sermon title or a word he spoke that night I do have an abiding awareness of the words 'Do not be deceived, God is not mocked' repeatedly echoing through my consciousness and the 'fear of God' coming upon me. I recognised that on Sundays I would acknowledge an act as sinful but by Wednesday and Thursday I would argue that it was not. I realised that I was fooling around with God, making Him my playmate. I was mocking Him by my foolishness.

To miss the mark – the essence of sin – does not change from Sunday to Monday, or according to the weather or your personal disposition. That night the 'fear of God' came on me in relation to a specific issue in my life. I can confidently say that I never had the need to indulge in that sinful activity since. I wish I could say that about all sin in my life.

I did, however, learn an important lesson that night. The fear of God – hating sin and having a respect for the holiness of God - becomes a roadblock to sin. In fact, it helps me to deal with temptation and to avoid sinning in the first place. To that end I constantly choose to walk in the fear of God but also pray and ask God to put liberal doses of the fear of God on me.

I monitor how much I fear God by my response to the promptings and conviction of the Holy Spirit. How long does it take me to obey Him? If I hesitate too long or try to negotiate a way out of it, then I am not honouring and respecting God. Is my obedience immediate and complete or is it delayed and partial? This is helpful when it comes to dealing with temptation and responding to conviction, but applies equally to being committed to obedience out of love and respect for God.

My Reaction to Temptation

When temptation comes, do I immediately resist the temptation or do I try to justify it and find excuses?

We were created for holiness. Sin was never part of our original design. As new creations in Christ, redeemed from our past guilt and shame, we don't have to sin in thought and word and deed every day. With discernment and sensitivity to the Holy Spirit, we can resist sinning at the level of temptation. Jesus as a man was tempted in every way that we will ever be but without sin.

An adequate respect for the holiness of God always results in an immediate rejection of temptation and taking the way of escape that is provided. Resisting temptation acts as a roadblock to sinning. Every time we resist temptation with sincerity and the fear of God, it leaves. It might return in a few minutes or hours or days but then we resist it again and it leaves.

After Jesus was baptized in the Jordan River He went into the wilderness 'full of the Holy Spirit' (Luke 4:1). He was specifically tempted by the devil on three occasions and resisted the devil by quoting the truth of the Word of God. After forty days of prayer and fasting He returned 'in the power of the Spirit' to Galilee (Luke 4:14). I recognise that, although being Spirit-filled doesn't make me immune to temptation, I can take courage from the fact that the Spirit does make me sensitive to it. Every time I successfully resist temptation, it builds my character and strengthens my spiritual muscles.

This might seem like an over-simplification but the three areas in which Jesus was tempted can be summarized in the following way. The first temptation had to do with meeting a legitimate need in the wrong way. Jesus was tempted to turn rocks into bread to satisfy His hunger. We are often tempted to satisfy our basic need for nourishment in greedy or selfish ways.

The second has to do with presumption, doing our own thing and expecting God to bail us out. Jesus was tempted to jump off the top of the temple and presume that God would rescue Him. This temptation is to do things without enquiring of God and assuming that He has our back.

The last temptation is about compromise - taking short cuts to avoid doing what we know is right. Jesus was tempted to acknowledge (worship) Satan and avoid going to the cross to regain authority over the nations. We will be tempted to set aside our moral convictions momentarily, to obtain short term results, without realising the long-term consequences.

I try to be continually alert to these temptations. The devil still uses these same tactics today to tempt us and we can equally overcome him by the power of the Word of God as Jesus did.

My Response to Conviction

Do I welcome the conviction of the Holy Spirit? How long does it take me to respond to the persuasion of the Holy Spirit when I have stepped out of line? If I respond immediately then I have a good measure of respect for God and His holiness. The longer it takes me to respond, the less of the 'fear of God' is on me.

Sin is contrary to our design and thus is both damaging to us and others. When we sin, we are living a lie and not the truth of who we really are. We should only tolerate sin in our lives for as long as it takes the Holy Spirit to convict us, and that is usually immediate. When we realize we have sinned we should deal with it immediately, and return to living the truth of who we really are.

I can write of many instances where I did respond to conviction immediately but also of others where I did not, and in some cases where there was a considerable delay in me acting. Most of the times when I responded quickly it was over an issue between God and me. Usually when there was a significant interval, it was because someone else was involved. And it was not always that I had to apologize or put something right. Even at times when I needed to share a word of affirmation or encouragement, I would hesitate.

Why the delay? I realized that I was more concerned with the opinions of the people involved than God's opinion of me. That is simply 'fear of man' – an over-developed concern for what people think. Rather than living for the smile of approval of God, I wanted to please people. That boils down to 'respecting' people more than 'respecting' God or having more of the 'fear of man' than the 'fear of God'. It is obvious then that a good measure of the fear of God in our lives can set us free from the fear of man.

When the Holy Spirit convicts us it is always unambiguous, loving and kind, albeit firm and convincing. This is because God is for us and not against us; He loves us and wants the best for us.

Condemnation is the opposite, as it comes from the enemy of our souls and is always accusatory, vague, and general. We do not have to listen to or submit to condemnation. The Bible also categorically states in Romans 8:1 that 'there is no condemnation for those that are in Christ Jesus'. This understanding has helped me to welcome the conviction of the Holy Spirit in my life and to be sensitive to His guidance.

Cecilia and I were sitting on a couch in our living room trying to have a conversation. When you have four active children in the house it is difficult to complete a sentence, let alone have a decent conversation, without being interrupted. John, then about ten years old, burst into the room and disturbed our moment of tranquillity. Cecilia asked him about something she had told him to do that he had ignored. His response to her was disrespectful and downright rude. I reacted in an improper way. Without thinking and with no hesitation I slapped him. He burst out crying and Cecilia was utterly shocked. I immediately told him to go to his room, as I needed to talk to him. The Holy Spirit had convicted me so quickly that as my hand was travelling through the air I knew I was doing the wrong thing. I should have stopped mid-air and withdrawn my hand but unfortunately followed through with the improper conduct.

I went for a walk through the house for a minute or two to regain my composure and went to John's room. He was sitting on his bed with big bewildered eyes probably wondering what I was going to do next. I knelt in front of him and acknowledged that I had acted inappropriately in slapping him and asked him to forgive me. He sighed a big sigh of relief. I pointed out that we had an agreed system of discipline in our home, which I had not followed and thus violated him. I also explained that I was not condoning his disobedience and especially not the way he spoke to his mother. I insisted that no one speaks to my wife like that. But what I did was equally wrong. We forgave each other were reconciled and prayed together.

I am not relating this story to tell you what a great humble dad I am but rather to illustrate that in that moment I feared God much more than I 'feared' my son. As a result, I was able to respond immediately to the conviction of the Holy Spirit out of honour and respect for God.

By the way, we had a 3D approach to discipline. We disciplined our children for the following three things only: disobedience, dishonesty and disrespect – that covered about any undesirable behaviour.

I could also tell you stories in which adults were involved – not that I go around slapping adults against the head - it is usually a lot subtler than that. I would be convicted to apologise for something and it would sometimes take me a week or two to do so. Why? Because I was more concerned by what the people thought of me than with what God thought of me. In other words, I feared man more than I feared God.

I was once on a trip to Cyprus via London for a missions conference. Afterwards I was going on a ministry trip to Dublin and then Belfast. On the flight from London to Larnaca in Cyprus my colleague asked me if I had a ticket to Belfast. I said yes! Which was not true because I had a ticket to Dublin. I was immediately convicted of the misinformation and instead of correcting it straight away I started justifying it as a small matter. He probably didn't care if I was going to Dublin or Belfast first. He probably wanted to help me financially if I hadn't bought a ticket yet.

It took me the good part of seven days before I raised the subject again. I have learnt that the longer you wait in such matters the more difficult it becomes. When I did eventually apologise for the misinformation his reaction was as predicted. No big deal. He just wanted to know if I had a ticket to either Dublin or Belfast. But that's not the point. The point is – was I more concerned with what God thinks of me than what man thinks of me? Did I fear God more than I feared man?

I am convinced that we are created for holiness and living in an open harmonious relationship with God. Sin is contrary to our original design and foreign or alien to who we really are. We do not have to sin in thought and word and deed every day. In fact, we needn't sin at all. Sin can be stopped at the level of temptation. And if we should sin it ought to be very seldom and only be part of our lives for as long as it takes the Holy Spirit to convict us. And that would be immediate. Our response should be just as instantaneous to ensure we keep 'short accounts' with God and live with confidence from a clear conscience.

oOo

Chapter 7
The Power of Forgiveness

Do not judge, and you will not be judged.
Do not condemn, and you will not be
condemned. Forgive, and you
will be forgiven.
Luke 6:37

Resentment is like drinking poison and
then hoping it will kill your enemies.
Nelson Mandela

The Power of Forgiveness

In 1974 Cecilia and I had the honour and special treat of sitting under the teaching of Tante Corrie ten Boom, a Dutch lady, in Amsterdam. The Nazis had imprisoned Corrie and her sister Betsie in February 1944 for sheltering Jews in their home. On her deathbed Betsie famously told Corrie, 'There is no pit so deep that God is not deeper still'. Betsie died on 16 December 1944. Corrie was miraculously released from the Ravensbruck concentration camp in Germany on 28 December that year due to a 'clerical error', one week before the entire group of women her age was exterminated.

We were both deeply touched by Corrie's ministry and her story of forgiveness. She told of how she was in Munich in 1947 speaking on forgiveness and was approached by the prison guard who had caused them so much pain and humiliation. He had since become a Christian and asked her to forgive him. She shared how she hesitated as all the painful memories came flooding back to her and how she was able to draw on the grace of God and choose to forgive her former enemy. They grasped each other's hands, the former guard and the former prisoner. She shared how she had never known God's love so intensely as she did then.

I have learnt that you can forgive anybody, anything that they have done to you if you really want to. And not only can you forgive, you must forgive. If you don't you will be trapped in the agonisingly more painful and restricting prison that results from bitterness and resentment.

Virtue is an attitude of heart, an act of the will rather than an emotion or feeling. We all know the saying 'patience is a virtue'. That's because patience is a choice and not a feeling. The emotion of patience follows the deliberate act of the will to be patient and not the other way around. Like any virtue, forgiveness is a choice not a feeling. If you wait until you feel like forgiving someone, you will wait a long time. As Corrie ten Boom affirms, 'Forgiveness is an act of the will, and the will can function regardless of the temperature of the heart.'

Along with a reverential respect for God's holiness, and an intrinsic hatred for sin and its consequences, an understanding of the power of forgiveness is another effective tool in my spiritual toolbox to assist me in living with a clear conscience.

Imprisoned by Resentment

In June 1978 Cecilia and I boarded a South African Airways flight in Buenos Aires for a flight to Cape Town. We had just completed a month of ministry in Argentina during 'Mundial', the Football World Cup. We were handed newspapers with front-page news of twelve Elim missionaries who had been massacred in the Vumba Mountains in Zimbabwe. We read name after name and saw gruesome photographs of people we knew personally and had worked alongside. Among them the picture of Joyce holding the hand of three-week-old Pamela, both savagely beaten to death. The sheer brutality of the event shocked us to the core. We were, in fact, scheduled to be with them in another few weeks with an outreach team from South Africa. I reacted with bitterness, anger, and resentment in my heart. Emotionally and spiritually it was one of my most unpleasant and longest flights home.

Back at the YWAM base I went through the routine of preparing the YWAM team for our outreach to Zimbabwe but I had no anointing or spiritual authority to do so. I remember publicly having to renounce my bitterness and resentment and declaring that I was willing to forgive my friends' murderers and if I should meet them I wanted to be able to minister the love of God to them. Only then was I free to lead the team again spiritually and to prepare for our time of ministry in Zimbabwe.

During the funeral service, Ron Chapman had prayed for the families of those who had been killed. He also prayed for those who were responsible for the killings. The theme at the funerals and at the memorial services all over the UK was 'Father forgive them'. Wow! What a powerful testimony.

In the booklet VUMBA - A Summary of the Tragedy published by the Elim International Missions Centre we read the following report. 'Rumours began to circulate in the early 1980s that several of the men personally responsible for the killings had been dramatically converted. Peter Griffiths was able to confirm the remarkable story of what happened to a group in the platoon who were together in an army camp shortly after the war had ended. Eight of them experienced a vision in which they saw the cross and the hand of God coming against them in judgment. Seven of them who had passports immediately left the country and enrolled in Bible Schools in West and East Africa. The other, not having a passport went to a Bible School in Harare. In another separate incident, an African pastor, working for Harare Intercessors, was asked to speak at a rehabilitation centre for ex-combatants. While he was preaching, a paraplegic man screamed out in agony out of deep conviction, crying for mercy. He later confessed that he had been one of those responsible for killing the missionaries. He told the pastor how the missionaries had prayed for their killers as they were being slaughtered.'

I only became aware of these reports years after the incident. It confirmed the initial conviction in my heart to forgive the perpetrators of that hideous atrocity and challenged me anew to guard my heart against bitterness and resentment. Mostly, though, I was filled with wonder and amazement at how the power and grace of God is released when we forgive those 'who know not what they do'.

Falsely Accused

April 26 1994 was a historic day for The Republic of South Africa. It officially marked the end of apartheid and the end of the old South Africa. The next day ushered in a three-day General Election period in which there would be 'universal adult suffrage' - citizens of all races being able to vote for the first time. That evening the old South African flag, which had been in use since 1928, was lowered for the last time to make room for the new flag of the emerging 'rainbow nation' to be hoisted in the morning.

Instead of being in South Africa to witness this significant transition I was in the neighbouring country of Namibia. The next day I was to answer to false accusations in the High Court. I was irritated to say the least and resented the waste of three precious days of my time especially during this momentous and pivotal season in my home county. A month before, I had received notification from the Registrar of the High Court in Namibia that the inquest into a murder was about to commence and that YWAM in general and I, in particular, were implicated. The accusations referred to the assassination of advocate Anton Lubowski an anti-apartheid activist and member of the South West African People's Organization (SWAPO). He was gunned down outside his house one evening by operatives of the Civil Cooperation Bureau (CCB) in September 1989 more than four years earlier.

I initially presumed I was implicated because one of the accused, an Irishman, had rented the YWAM guest facilities under the guise of being a journalist. However, after enquiring as to how we were implicated I was sent the affidavit of a policeman who had attended a Discipleship Training School (DTS) in Windhoek from June to December 1988 who was a co-accused in the murder. In a five-page affidavit he implicated me in the plot to assassinate Labowski. He alleged that I was a commander in the South African Defence Force, that I posed to be a clergyman and that I trained people in espionage, information gathering, and surveillance and that YWAM was involved in subversive activity.

The irony of the matter was that I had not lived in Namibia since 1983 and only visited a few times a year. I had only spoken in the specific DTS referred to for a few days on subjects like Being Real, Integrity, Humility, Submission, Self-Worth, The Fatherheart of God, Relinquishment of Rights and Being Salt and Light in the Community.

Initially when this was brought to my attention I thought it was a big joke. However, when the investigating officer asked me to submit an affidavit to answer the indictments I realised that it wasn't such a laughing matter after all. I could submit an affidavit refuting the allegations and detailing my activities during the few days in question in Namibia including flight numbers, titles of lectures and so on. When I was later subpoenaed to appear in the High Court of Namibia, within three days, I realised it was much more serious than I had anticipated. Both my integrity and the reputation of YWAM were at stake. I was frustrated as well as apprehensive and annoyed.

In the Dock

The twenty minutes or so in the dock were awkward, reasonably uncomfortable, slightly humiliating, and greatly humbling. There was also a moment of total panic offset by great relief.

Immediately after my affidavit had been read and verified I was expecting to be cross-examined about the alleged clandestine training I had given and my supposed identity as an army officer. I was caught off-guard by questions from the judge's chair rather than from an attorney on the floor. I was also naïve in terms of court procedure calling the judge 'Your Honour' instead of 'Your Lordship,' to the amusement of my friends in the public gallery.

The first question from the judge was related to my affiliation to the CCB. I told the judge that I could not even consciously remember what the CCB stood for let alone being affiliated to them. He made a comment about my naïvety. It was showing.

The following few questions had to do with politics, my personal and the mission's views on Marxism and communism, and the conflict in Namibia. The court wanted to know if I, specifically, and the mission in general were anti-communist. I assured the court that we were apolitical and not anti-anything but pro-Christ and that we prayed for and worked for the peaceful solution in any conflict.

At one stage in the cross-examination the State Prosecutor asked me how I remembered all the detail of flight numbers and lecture titles that I submitted in my affidavit. After all, the few days in question at the DTS occurred almost four and a half years earlier. I produced my 1988 journal and explained that I keep a meticulous account of my travels, speaking engagements and corporate decisions for various reasons. Towards the end of the proceedings he referred again to my 1988 diary and asked, 'Can you tell the honourable Court where you were on 2 December 1988?' - the graduation day of the DTS in question.

I nonchalantly grabbed my journal and turned to the said date. It was blank. I momentarily froze with fright. In fact, the journal was blank for a few days on either side of that date. In my panic, I turned to the Year Planner and saw that I had booked out 1-17 December USA & Hawaii, International Strategy Conference. A moment of pure relief! I calmly passed that information on to the court.

The court very quickly realised that the accusations against me were ludicrous and that both the policeman attending a DTS and the Irish journalist had used YWAM as a front organisation. I was released to return to South Africa 'to take care of important business': to cast my vote in the South African General Elections the next day.

The next morning as I prepared for the flight home I was surprised that I made the 8 o'clock news headlines with Nelson Mandela. The first report was Mandela's comment about the unprecedented election starting later that day. The next report was of me refuting the allegations in the High Court, a small consolation after the accusatory newspaper headlines of the previous few days. I felt a little exonerated and somewhat vindicated. The scant report of my innocence did not appear on the front page of the newspapers that day.

But there was still an issue to be resolved. I had to deal with what I would have liked to call 'a slight reserve' in my heart towards the persons who had wronged me but let's call it what it is. Resentment! Bitterness! Unforgiveness! I felt violated and betrayed. Trust had been broken. My integrity and the reputation of the mission had been tainted.

I had to make the cold-blooded choice to forgive the individuals involved. Every time I review the incident I must reinforce that choice once again. Even now, more than twenty years later, I keep reminding myself that forgiveness is a constant ongoing attitude of the heart. In the spirit of openness, I must be honest, although the principle of forgiveness has been established in my life I still find it difficult to even contemplate having to trust again, those who slandered my character in such a public way.

Forgiveness and Trust

I forgive primarily for my sake. Now I know that sounds terribly selfish but I believe it is also wise and intelligent. It is my personal policy to be quick to forgive – for my sake. I don't want to be imprisoned by the irresponsible actions of others and definitely not by the schemes of a fallen angel and defeated enemy. To trust again takes time, though. Once trust has been violated it takes time, sometimes a long time, to be re-established. Rightly or wrongly my personal policy is to be quick to forgive but slow to trust.

It has been our joy over many years to see people's lives restored by the ministry of Jesus from a place of shame and devastation to beauty and wholeness. It is particularly difficult for people who have been physically and emotionally abused, especially by those close to them, to come to the place of forgiveness. When we have encouraged such folk to forgive those who have hurt them, almost without exception there has been a massive reluctance. The feeling has always been that if they forgive they are condoning what the person did. They are saying it is okay. Our counsel has always been that abuse is never okay. You are not condoning or excusing what the person did by forgiving them. But what you are doing is setting yourself free from the prison of resentment and the bondage of bitterness so that God can start the restoration process.

Imagine if someone stabbed a knife into my back. I would have one of two options. Either, I could hurry to someone to remove the blade and disinfect the wound. The healing process can then begin. Or, I could back up into a wall and repeatedly bang the protruding knife deeper and deeper into my body. Just the thought of that probably makes you cringe. But we do that spiritually. We allow issues of the past to become festering wounds by indulging in bitterness, resentment, unforgiveness, and hatred.

Allowing the person that you have forgiven access to you to keep on being abusive is another story. Be willing to forgive but be very careful to trust readily again. Trust needs to be earned.

Justice and Mercy

God is a compassionate God. He is a God of both justice and mercy. We also love both justice and mercy but we want justice for others - especially our enemies - and mercy for ourselves.

In 2002 I was driving through morning rush hour traffic in the inner city of Pretoria when I witnessed a smash and grab. I was stationary at a red traffic light, second car from the front. I saw a young man walk nonchalantly across the road in front of us to the car in the right turning lane, smash the passenger window, grab the handbag off the front seat, run back across the road, and disappear into a subway leading to a nearby station. The lights turned green and the traffic moved on as if nothing had happened.

I drove up onto the sidewalk at the entrance to the subway and was getting out of my car to run after the thief when it dawned on me how stupid that was. I was about to leave my car with the keys still in the ignition and the thief was probably waiting in the subway with a crowbar ready to bash my head in. I got back into my car slightly shaken and very irritated that petty crime like that could go on unchecked.

As I drove off I replayed the incident in my head. I wished that God had allowed me to be the front car at the intersection rather than the second one. I could then have dropped my clutch and knocked the guy over or at least pinned him to the nearby wall with my car. As I drove through the city that day on various errands, I was especially vigilant at each intersection, with the revs on my engine kept intentionally high, hoping to find a criminal that I could 'take out' at a moment's notice or the drop of a clutch. Fortunately, it never did happen.

A few weeks later our son John picked me up at the airport after I had been away on a ministry trip. He related an incident that morning of an attempted theft of Cecilia's car in the driveway at our home. I felt the irritation, frustration and anger rising in my heart. How dare that happen on my patch?

Back home Cecilia related the detail of the incident to me. She and Donovan had been out shopping and had intended to pay a utility bill but had left the documents at home. They quickly went home, parked in the driveway, popped indoors for a quick drink, and collected the papers. On returning outside they surprised a burglar who had already gained entrance to her car and was busy hotwiring it. The ignition lights were already on. Another minute or two later and the car would have been gone. The thief's getaway was so hasty that he left a brand-new pair of well-known 'name brand' trainers behind and made his retreat barefoot.

Of course, I was grateful that Cecilia and the children hadn't been harmed, and that the car hadn't been stolen, although it was damaged. But I was irritated and frustrated that it should even have taken place.

I pray for the protection of my family when I am away. Why did it happen? I felt agitated, frustrated, and somewhat angry.

The next morning as I was dismantling the damaged ignition switch to replace it I played through the incident in my mind. I wished it had happened while I was home. I imagined myself detecting the thief in the car and sneaking around the other side of the house. As he saw me and was about to get out of the car I would kick the door in, trapping his neck in the door. I would then make a citizen's arrest and duly tie up his hands and feet. I then imagined hanging him up by his feet from the tree in the front garden and calling the police with the hope that they would take hours to show up. Some of my friends would regard that as a very African vigilante-style approach to justice.

'You wanted justice for the handbag snatcher, didn't you?' I heard the still small voice of my conscience asking. 'Yes, yes, yes!' I retorted. 'What about the car thief? You want justice in his case as well, don't you?' 'Yes!' I thought. 'And if the police weren't going to do it then I better do it.' 'And what about you? Do you want justice for you?' I felt the gentle but firm conviction of the Holy Spirit. I knew God had me backed into a corner. 'No! Please not.' I pleaded. 'I need mercy.'

I wrestled with God. Why didn't He allow it to happen when I was home? Then I could have done something about it. Why did He allow it to happen at all? I felt God quietly convict me that it was because of my attitude. I didn't understand. I wasn't even home. I soon understood though that I had made my family and myself vulnerable because I wanted to execute justice and not show mercy.

And that is exactly the point. We want mercy for ourselves but justice for those we deem as enemies. Why? Because we think that we are on the right side of justice. We forget that God has given us another chance and another chance and another chance and that God has shown us mercy because justice has been served. It was served on Christ on our behalf and on behalf of all humanity, including our enemies.

Now I am not suggesting that we condone crime, violence, and injustice but we cannot respond to these things with a 'holier than thou' attitude. In chapter four of the book of James, it is clear that we should not judge others because only God has the right to judge (James 4:12). The question is not whether we are right or wrong in our judgement but who are we to judge, in the first place? Only God knows the up-to-date detail of every person's heart.

Family Inheritance

My father was the eldest of four siblings: two brothers and a sister. He always had hopes of inheriting the family farm as the first-born. Years before my grandfather's death he decided to apportion the inheritance, which I thought was very magnanimous of him. The problem was that my aunt inherited the farm and the sons each received a monetary inheritance equal to the value of the farm. My grandfather considered that completely fair and just.

Unfortunately, my dad reacted with bitterness and resentment and although I was not privy to all that went on it caused strained relationships in the family. I saw Dad stagnate spirituality and his health deteriorate. He was even starting to drink excessively. His excuse was that he was self-medicating because he couldn't sleep well. I tried to share my concerns with him and address the issue but with seemingly very little effect. I was reminded that even Jesus could do no miracles in his home town of Nazareth due to the people's familiarity and unbelief and alluded to a prophet being without honour in his hometown, among his relatives, and in his own household.

My dad has only called me long distance – internationally-twice in my life. The first time was to congratulate us at the news of our first child. The second time was a complete surprise. He told me that he had good news for me. My response was that it must be great news if he was calling me. He informed me that he had met with his brothers and sister and that they had resolved the issue over the inheritance. (My grandfather had already passed away, unfortunately). They had forgiven one another and were reconciled. He further shared with me that he felt like a 'new person'. Many of the physical ailments that he had been suffering from disappeared almost overnight. Again, this confirmed to me the power of forgiveness and the detrimental effect of resentment, not only spiritually and psychologically, but also physically.

Self-Recrimination

If you are anything like me there are probably some things you did or decisions you made that you wish you could undo. But we can't. I wish I could rewrite some of the chapters of my life especially the one related to my father in my teenage years, but I can't. That is water under the bridge. The clock cannot be turned back.

We can easily become self-incriminating and even resentful and bitter towards ourselves for these incidents. Self-resentment imprisons us as much as unforgiveness towards others does. We need to take responsibility for the issues, embrace the grace of God, and forgive ourselves. How do we do that? By repenting of and turning away from the self-resentment and self-blame involved.

In Genesis, Joseph understood this principle and the tendency of human nature to resent or hate ourselves when we have done wrong. When he finally revealed himself to his brothers after they had sold him into slavery twenty-two years previously he was quick to encourage them not to blame or resent themselves for what they had done, for God had used it for the good of them all (Gen 45:5).

On Sunday 27 September 1981 Loren and Darlene Cunningham flew into Windhoek, Namibia from Johannesburg to spend the day with us as a YWAM team. We arranged a special function where they could address the staff and students and 'friends of YWAM' in the City. Having the visionary leaders of the mission with us was such a significant event that I summoned the YWAMmers who were serving in remote areas of the country as teachers and nurses to join us for the weekend.

On the Friday afternoon Stephanie van der Poel, who had been serving as a teacher in Damaraland, was killed in a car accident on her way to the base. Mr Da Sousa the headmaster of the school where she was serving called that evening to break the news to me. He relayed the circumstances of her death, that she had died instantly, that her passenger was seriously injured and died shortly afterwards, where her body and belongings were being kept, and what police station I needed to contact. My head was spinning. I immediately blamed myself. If I hadn't insisted that she come for the day with the Cunninghams it would not have happened. It was my fault.

I went through the motion of contacting her pastor in Cape Town and asked him to go to her parents' home and call me from there. I was then able to break the news to them and share my condolences with them while he could pray with them and support them. All the while the sword of self-recrimination was hanging over my head.

On the Sunday morning, I broke the news to the Cunninghams in the VW van in the airport car park. Loren intuitively picked up my self-resentment and immediately started ministering to me. He encouraged me not to blame myself. We don't always need to understand these tragedies. We need to trust God in them. I remember us praying together that good would come out of it and being encouraged by the scripture 'unless a grain of wheat falls into the ground and dies, it remains alone; but if it dies, it produces much grain' (John 12:24b NKJV).

We had a great day with the Cunninghams despite the tragedy weighing heavily on our minds. On the Monday I went to retrieve Stephanie's belongings and to arrange for her body to be flown to Cape Town. Amongst her stuff was a cassette tape neatly packaged and addressed, ready to be mailed to her parents.

On Thursday that week I flew to Cape Town to be at the funeral. Her father Stephan, a strapping big man, met me at the airport. I was deeply struck by his slumped shoulders and bloodshot eyes. He embraced me with a bear hug and thanked me profusely for all we had done for their daughter. I told him I was so happy to hear that as I was concerned that he and his wife would blame me for recruiting her into missions and placing her in a remote place. He assured me that that was never in their mind and reprimanded me for even thinking so.

Back at their home I could share my condolences with Stephanie's mother and deliver her belongings including the cassette tape. We decided to listen to the tape immediately. The tape was an oral journal, recording events over the past few weeks. At one stage she told of the Cunninghams coming to visit Namibia and that I had requested she come to Windhoek for the weekend. She then added 'But I don't feel like going'. Ah! That was like a dagger to my soul re-enforcing my self-blame. I should never have asked her to come. It was my fault.

Stephanie continued to share the events that transpired over the next few days and then ended the tape on the evening of Thursday 24 September 1981 by saying she was now going to travel the 450 kilometres to Windhoek the following afternoon to be at the YWAM event for the weekend. She felt God prompt her to go because he had a special appointment with her. She ended the recording by saying 'Goodbye Mom and Dad. I am excited to discover what my appointment with Jesus is this weekend!' Her parents sobbed uncontrollably!

I went to the bathroom in an emotional state, looked myself in the mirror, said something to the effect that I didn't understand the events of the last week, and released myself from the blame. It was not my fault. If Stephanie, one of our best missionaries, had run her race, finished her work on earth, and been ushered into heaven, who was I to argue.

That evening I met with their pastor to confirm the plans for the funeral the next day. He introduced me to his daughter who had been living away from home in a rebellious state. On hearing of Stephanie's death she immediately returned home, was reconciled with her parents, and recommitted her life to Christ. There was already fruit from the seed that had fallen in the ground.

The next day, as I was walking out of the church behind the coffin a young lady, Stephanie's age, joined me. She shared how she and Stephanie had worked together on a Kibbutz in Israel and had both felt the call to missions. She felt that Stephanie had answered that call and had already finished her task whereas she had not even responded yet. She asked if she could replace Stephanie. Within months she was serving as a missionary teacher in Damaraland, Namibia. More fruit! And I am sure there was a lot more.

Forgiving God

I remember a young man being brought to me by his spiritual leader for prayer and advice regarding a problem he had with trusting God. He was known in the community for resenting God for having lost his dad when he was young. Often when things went wrong in his life, instead of taking responsibility, he would blame it on losing his father when he was young.

I didn't even bother to sit down for a long drawn out counselling and prayer session. I stood over him and said, 'You don't need me to resolve this issue. You can do it by yourself. All you need to do is forgive God.' You could see the question mark form on his forehead. 'Forgive God?' he questioned. 'I can't forgive God. God doesn't sin!'

'Exactly!' I replied. I could see the light come into his eyes and the understanding dawn on him. God was not to blame.

Now, technically we can't forgive God, but we can deal with the resentment and bitterness in our heart towards Him by asking Him to forgive us for resenting Him. We often blame God for things He is not responsible for, and are imprisoned by it.

My Mantra

My mantra on forgiveness is simply this: You can and you must. If you don't you won't.

You can forgive anybody anything they have done to you if you really want to because it is a choice and not a feeling. You not only can forgive; you must forgive because if you don't you won't be free. You'll be imprisoned by a defeated fallen angel's schemes and someone else's indiscretion. Don't allow it to happen!

oOo

Chapter 8
Humility

Have this attitude in yourselves which was also in Christ Jesus....
Being found in appearance as a man, He humbled Himself by
becoming obedient to the point of death, even death on a cross.
Philippians 2:5,8 (NASB)

True humility is not thinking less of yourself;
it is thinking of yourself less.
C.S. Lewis

My initial view of humility was one of feebleness and weakness, of being bashful and shy, of timidity and paleness, of feelings of insecurity and insignificance. Nothing could be further from the truth. Jesus was humble but He was none of these things. The definition of humility that I heard often after I embarked on my discipleship journey and that has impacted my life the most is: Humility is a willingness to be known for who you really are!

First, it is willingness as an attitude of heart as much as an act of the will. You don't go around wearing a label on your forehead that says 'humility' or 'pride', but it is an internal attitude. God is not impressed with our outward appearance or demeanour. He looks at the heart.

Secondly, it is a willingness to be known for who you really are. Not who you think you are, or who you want other people to think you are, or even who you think others think you are, but who you really are. That deepened my resolve to be set free from any facade or trappings of pretence to be the real me.

I discovered that while it was relatively easy (I say relatively because it was still difficult initially) to acknowledge my failures, weaknesses, and mistakes I found it very difficult to acknowledge any positive attribute or characteristic about myself or to embrace any positive recognition or affirmation from others. I came to the place where I was willing to acknowledge the negative stuff but found it difficult to embrace the positive. I had subconsciously learnt that to be positive and affirming of myself was wrong. That it was proud and arrogant and sinful to do so. I only saw humility as embracing the negative aspects of my life. I was, at best, only being half humble. I guess half humility means half pride and pride is pride that keeps us in bondage and suppresses us into the superficial realm of pretence. Pride is the smokescreen between being artificial and being real.

Every time I have told an audience that I was going to do an exercise to prove to them that they were, at best, only fifty percent humble, I would get a few uneasy chuckles. When I asked them to tell one another three positive and affirming things about themselves they would become uncomfortable. There would be a nervous tension in the room and a few anxious looks. Very few would respond enthusiastically. Why? Because we have believed the lie that to be positive and affirming of ourselves is to be proud. We have assumed that it is downright sinful and wrong to do so. Let me suggest that is not true.

When I then asked them to turn to one another and to share some of their failures, sins, and mistakes most found it a lot easier. Now it takes humility to be open and honest about the negative aspects of your life but it takes as much if not more humility to acknowledge and embrace the positive aspects of your life and character.

Humility cuts both ways – both negatively and positively. If that is who you really are then to recognise it in all honesty and with the right attitude is an act of humility. If it is true, then it is humble to acknowledge it. Humility is honest. Humility agrees with God. Humility embraces the truth of who you really are. Pride denies the truth of who you really are and believes a lie.

To my relief, I realised that although Jesus was the model and ultimate example of humility He was very comfortable with His identity and had no inferiority complex. In fact, He made some radical statements about Himself: 'I am The Way, The Truth and The Life; I am The Door; I am The Good Shepherd; I am The Bread of Life; I am The Fountain of Living Water; I am The Light of the World; no one comes to The Father except through Me'. There is not one iota of pride or arrogance in these statements because they are all true. That's who He really is. He is the personification of true humility. Humility speaks the truth; it agrees with God; it is honest.

Humility is Not Inferiority

For too long I equated humility with inferiority. I thought to bashfully cower away in shyness was a very humble thing to do. That is a lie of the enemy. In fact, inferiority or false modesty is based in pride. It is a reversed or fabricated form of humility which is nothing other than pride because that is not who we really are. It is a lie that any of us are inferior to anyone else. To believe that we are is based in an untruth and is inverted pride.

To suffer from inferiority, lack of self-love, a low self-image or self-esteem - name it what you will - is to deny who you really are. To reject who you are is the height of arrogance and pride. A lack of self-acceptance says to the most wonderful creator, the wisest designer, the most loving sculptor, the most exquisite developer, that He did not do a good job when He made you. What could be more proud and arrogant than that?

We are all unique, a one-of-a-kind person, and will never be more valuable or less valuable to God than we are right now. We don't measure our value or worth by our appearance or performance. We are valuable and precious because God created us as such and assigned that value to us.

Humility is Not a Spirit of Comparison

Looking back over more than forty years of ministry now, and our involvement mostly with young people, we have found that the overwhelming majority of those struggling with feelings of inferiority and self-acceptance issues also struggle with a 'spirit of comparison'. They have an obsession to compare themselves with others or live under the expectations of continually being compared with others by parents or grandparents or other significant people in their lives.

When I say 'spirit of comparison' I do not mean a demonic spirit but an attitude or pre-disposition to always compare oneself with others to determine where you fit in the pecking order. Paul the Apostle writes to the church in Corinth and warns them that they are unwise or foolish in comparing themselves with one another. He never says that it is sinful to do so. He just says that it is stupid and unnecessary to do so.

There is only one person that we compare ourselves with and that is Jesus. He is the perfect example of us. He is our prototype. He is the one that we are designed to be like. Whenever we compare ourselves with Jesus we are never left feeling inferior or condemned but rather encouraged and affirmed to be who we are created to be. We have seen literally hundreds of young people set free from inferiority by renouncing a 'spirit of comparison' and replacing it with the truth of God's unconditional love for them and the acceptance of their true identity in Christ.

Humility is not Weakness

Humility doesn't say 'I cannot' but rather 'I need God'. This is especially important for men to grasp because the prevailing perception of manliness is the antithesis of humility. The general worldview of manliness or being macho is that of pride and arrogance and abrasiveness. Nothing can be further from the truth. You will never be a real man, a man of God, without true humility. It takes more guts and tenacity to swim upstream than just to float downstream with all the filth and junk around you. Humility is a strong moral characteristic, not a weakness.

Meekness is not weakness. We get the picture of meekness from a wild stallion that has been tamed and adequately trained. A little girl who knows something about horse riding can mount the former wild stallion and control its movements by manipulating the bit and the bridle. What is the difference between the wild stallion and the tame stallion? Has it lost any of its strength or speed? No! The only difference is that its strength is now under control. It has been yielded to the bit and the bridle. Meekness is not weakness; it is strength under control, a yielded will. Humility yields to God. Jesus is humble but He is not a weakling!

Humility is not Timidity

We are not to confuse humility with cowardice. In the first chapter of the book of Timothy, Paul writes to his prodigy and explains that God has not given us a spirit of timidity or cowardice but rather one of boldness. We don't have to be shy with the gifts God has given us or of who He made us to be. We don't have to be intimidated by the opinions of others or fear what they think of us.

Humility is to be loving and sensible. It is to have sound judgement and live a disciplined life of self-control. The Spirit empowers us to do so. Humility is thus not to be shy or bashful or to be intimidated by the opinions of others but to fully embrace who we are.

Humility is not Insecurity

Confidence and humility are not contradictory. We saw in Chapter Six that true confidence is developed in our character and is not just a skin-deep personality trait. A lack of confidence, sense of inadequacy or insecurity have got nothing to do with humility. It is also a misconception that to be confident in who you are and to be comfortable in your skin, so to speak, is to be proud. To be well-trained and to be functioning well in your abilities, gifts, and talents has nothing to do with being proud. That's who you are! It would be arrogant and prideful to think that you achieved these traits independently of God and others.

In my approximately 500 flying hours as a private pilot there are two occasions when I was forced to make a precautionary landing in a remote area due to mist blanketing my destination airport. In both cases I had been flying the type of aircraft, a Piper Cherokee 180 (PA28-180), almost on a weekly basis. I was so familiar with the aircraft that it felt like part of me – an extra limb if you will - and had already landed numerous times on roads in a refugee camp or adjacent to a mission station that I visited regularly. Plus, in preparation for my annual flight tests, I would rehearse the procedures for forced landings and precautionary landings thoroughly. In addition, I always acknowledged my dependence on God before every flight and entrusted myself and any passengers and the aircraft to Him, although I had done it many times before.

In both these situations I was able to fly the pattern for selecting a suitable landing spot: execute a safe landing in a sugar cane field in the one instance and on a narrow farm road in the other. I subsequently could take off again safely once the mist had cleared, having initially selected a landing spot that would enable me to do so. Of course, God helped me and protected my passengers and me. But this was not independent of the instructors that had instilled these skills in me, me using them to the best of my ability, and committing them to God and trusting Him to help me execute them confidently.

Humility is not Insignificance

In my pre-teenage years, my dad and I (my dad really) were building a caravan for our family holidays. We spent most of our Saturdays, when I was not playing soccer, and many evenings on this project. My dad was a proficient sheet metal worker and very meticulous about the aluminium cladding being perfect both outside and inside the caravan. He would allow me to hold things for him and even pass tools to him but never to do anything of significance, like cut a piece of aluminium or fix it into position. It was only months into the project that he would allow me to drill a hole, under close scrutiny, and shoot in the pop rivet. Sometimes he would ask me for a specific tool but before I could find it he would rush past me impatiently, grab it, and get on with the job. I was left feeling belittled and insignificant. These feelings of unimportance fuelled my inferiority and confusion over true and false humility.

Despite that - or maybe because of it - I developed a desire to work with my hands and to be creative, practically. I was given that opportunity through a man in our church, Harry Barnes. He ran a small blacksmith and welding workshop as a 'home industry' where he created an environment for teenage boys to learn practical skills and earn pocket money on Saturdays and during their school holidays.

By the age of sixteen I was a proficient welder, able to earn significant pocket money in my spare time. When I turned eighteen I could buy my first car from the savings. Being able to manufacture wrought iron furniture; security doors and grills; steel gates and fencing contributed significantly to my budget as a student. Those skills have stood me in good stead ever since.

Harry Barnes became my father-in-law. After working alongside him and later in partnership with him for seven years he felt confident enough to entrust his eldest daughter, Cecilia, to me to be my wife.

To this day I have a fondness for DIY projects and working with tools. Hardly a Saturday goes by that I don't find some project, big or small, to get my teeth into or rather lay my hands on. It always gives me a sense of satisfaction and fulfilment to see a job well done. At this stage in life I would hope that it is much more than fulfilling a need but rather a celebration of who I am.

Humility Depends on God

One lesson that I have learnt repeatedly is my total dependence on God. Humility acknowledges our deep need of God in everything we do every day even if we have done it successfully many times before. The danger is to presume on the blessing and favour of God and to act independently of Him. Both presumption and independence are based in pride. The Bible is clear that pride precedes a fall: 'Pride goes before destruction, and a haughty spirit before a fall' (Proverbs 16:18).

Before Jesus taught His disciples how to pray He told them that our Heavenly Father knows our needs even before we ask Him, yet He taught them to pray and ask for their daily provision – 'give us this day our daily bread'. He was teaching them to acknowledge their need of Him and their total dependence on Him as their Father, daily. That is humility.

To presume on God's provision and to take His blessings for granted is based in arrogance and pride. Humility acknowledges need, confidently asks, and then patiently trusts. Constant gratitude for God's daily provision is an expression of humility. Conversely, a lack of thankfulness is based in pride.

I have had the privilege of teaching certain subjects dozens, if not hundreds, of times. Every time I have the opportunity to teach or preach, whether a familiar subject or a new one, I do the possible in terms of prayer and preparation and still acknowledge my deep need of God to help me in my inadequacies and anoint His word. Without this dependent humility, it is impossible to truly trust God.

While we dependently trust God in humility we also need to humbly acknowledge that God depends on us to co-operate with Him and trusts us to walk in His ways. We honour God by humbling ourselves before Him. He in turn honours us with His favour and grace.

Humility is Interdependent

God never created us to be self-sufficient and to go through life as 'lone rangers'. We were created for relational living and interdependence. Humility has the attitude 'I need you: please help me' while at the same time recognising and asking, 'You need me: how can I help you?' Humility is interdependent with others. Humility is an acknowledgement that we need one another and are mutually dependent on one another. Just as independence from God is based in pride, so an attitude of independence from others is based in pride.

The independence that I am referring to here is of course not independence in terms of maturity but rather the independent attitude or spirit that infers that we don't need God or others. Interdependence based in humility implies a healthy mature independence with a mutual dependence on others in the Body of Christ for the sake of spiritual growth.

I have found that many of my spiritual or emotional needs are met in my relationship with God, but not all of them. It is as if God reserves the right to meet some of our needs through the 'Jesus' in others rather than directly by Himself. It is often only when I have acknowledged the need of others that solutions have come.

There have been times when I have been open and vulnerable with colleagues or friends with a need in my life that I have experienced the grace of God being activated even before they have prayed with me or advised me on the issue. At other times, it needed their counsel, prayer, and intervention.

The Bible is clear that we are members of a body, Christ's body, and that the members of a body need each other. We cannot function independently of one another or separate from the body. God would violate that principle if He took care of all our needs directly without allowing many of the needs in the body to be met by the Body of Christ ministering to one another.

Humility Takes Responsibility

Pride shifts the blame but humility takes responsibility.

The problem started way back in Genesis in the Garden of Eden when Adam and Eve ate the fruit that God prohibited them from eating. When God confronted Adam he did not take responsibility for his disobedience but shifted the blame to Eve directly and God indirectly for making her in the first place. When God challenged Eve she in turn passed the buck by blaming the serpent for enticing her to do it. (The serpent, in turn, had no leg to stand on.)

In Chapter Six I referred to an incident where I had to apologise to my son for wrongly disciplining him. Apart from responding to the conviction of the Holy Spirit out of respect for Him, in humility I had to take responsibility for my wrong action. My children know that I am not perfect but they have also learnt that you take responsibility for your wrong actions.

There have been times as a leader that I have had to apologise for wrong decisions or take responsibility for a messy situation. The temptation is always to hold back from owning up out of fear of rejection or diminished respect. Exactly the opposite is true. There is freedom in acknowledging failure and taking responsibility. Humility does not imply perfection but it does imply honesty, authenticity, and integrity.

Humility Activates the Grace of God

'God resists the proud, but gives grace to the humble'.
James 4:6 (NKJV)

The grace of God is abundant and free. It is as infinite as a shoreless ocean. It is available to every person on earth but it is not automatic. It is triggered by humility – the simple acknowledgement that we need God and that we need others.

I need the enabling grace of God in everything I do every day of my life. The Bible is emphatic that God resists the proud but gives grace to the humble. There are enough things in life that resist us and what we want to do for God without making it more difficult for ourselves by being proud and independent. I have learnt, often the hard way, that God has no qualms about setting up roadblocks for me. He is much more committed to my character than my comfort. He will make things difficult for me, if needs be, for me to humble myself so that

He can in turn bless me and activate His grace over my life. Wow! What a loving God.

When we humble ourselves before God and turn away from sin – repentance – and acknowledge Jesus as Lord in our life, the grace of salvation and God's forgiveness is released. Similarly, when we humbly acknowledge our dependence on God and need of Him in taking care of our daily responsibilities, then enabling grace comes to empower us do what we need to do.

It has been my and Cecilia's experience through difficult times, whether that be physical illness or financial struggles or ministry challenges, that humility always activates the abundant grace of God. Paul the apostle asked God three times to rid him of some besetting problem. God's reply to him was, 'My grace is sufficient for you, for my power is made perfect in your weakness' (2 Corinthians 12:9). That has been our testimony over and over again.

Just as it is crazy to think that we can be saved by our own human efforts, it is as great a fallacy to think that we can go through difficult times in our own strength without the grace of God. As we humbly acknowledge that before God, His grace is activated to help us go through the storms of life.

oOo

Chapter 9
Openness

Jesus said 'I am the light of the world.
Whoever follows me will never walk in
darkness, but will have the light of life'.
John 8:12

Openness is an attitude of heart. It is a willingness to come
out of hiding with the sins and needs in our life,
before those spiritually involved in our life,
so that those things can be dealt with.
It is simply 'living in the light'.

Talking about being real, the question is: 'Who are you really?' The answer is actually quite simple. You are your secrets. What you hide is who you really are. If you are taking refuge behind a barrier or wearing a mask or having to pretend in any way, you are hiding who you really are. What you then project into the realm of reality is not the real you but a pretend you. If, on the other hand, you have no secrets and nothing to hide then what you project into the realm of reality is the real you. Now, that's the way to live.

I am the most comfortable and relaxed with the people who I have been the most open and vulnerable with - those who have seen me at my best and at my worst.

By openness I don't mean finding a room full of people and arbitrarily spouting out all your needs and sins and failures for all and sundry to hear. What I do mean, however, is that you must be willing to be open with, and accountable to, a few people with whom you have a relationship of trust. In other words, you bring any issues to the light in a responsible manner. Once you have done that the principle of living in the light has been established. You are no longer defined by your secrets. You are free to be who you really are without pretending anything.

We have been conditioned to smile when we feel like crying; to laugh when things aren't so funny at all; to respond glibly with 'Fine!' when we are asked: 'How are you?', although we might not be fine at all. This is pretense and hides who we really are. Why do we do this?

I don't know about you but I don't like getting hurt physically or emotionally. When there is any pending danger our reaction is to shield ourselves from it. If we have been hurt in relationships in the past, it is natural to keep people at arm's length when forming new relationships. This is to protect ourselves from getting hurt again. Although this is a self-protection mechanism it does result in us building a castle around us to retreat into and leaves us with superficial, shallow relationships with others.

Letting others into our lives does make us vulnerable, but I have found that the reward that comes with 'being real' far outweighs the risk.

Trying to project an image that is not truly us or being locked into the perceptions and expectations of others can be taxing. Certain images are conjured up in our minds when we hear titles like policeman, teacher, housewife, lawyer, salesman, rock star, banker, minister or missionary. These titles are stereotyped, as are the different roles we might be in, and carry with them assumed characteristics and predictable behaviour. Striving to live up to these expectations or even pretending to fit the mould, can be burdensome.

While we should be professional and excellent at our occupations we should not let the image of our job or the title associated with it define our identity and hide our true identity - who we really are.

As a young adult, and then as a trainee missionary or 'apprentice', I had several heroes of the faith that I was striving to emulate. The problem with striving to be like others is that you are left drained. You burn up a lot of emotional and spiritual capital that you could better invest in being yourself.

Openness is the basis of true meaningful fellowship with God. God doesn't want to fellowship with the pretend you, He wants to fellowship with the real you. The only way for that to happen is for you to live in the light – out in the open.

I once noticed a group of eight-year-old girls with things stuffed under their clothes to simulate having big tummies. I asked them what they were doing and they said they were 'playing hospital'. They were pretending to be pregnant. A while later they walked by me again each carrying a doll wrapped in a baby blanket. They had played at giving birth. To my relief, it was only a charade - only a game. God doesn't play games with us. He doesn't want to fellowship with the pretend you He wants the real you.

Sin hides and light reveals. The first thing that happened when Adam and Eve sinned is that they hid from God and true meaningful fellowship was broken. When God came into the garden in the evening for the customary fellowship with His creation and asked 'Adam, where are you?' It was not a geographical question but a spiritual one. He knew where Adam and Eve were hiding. That wasn't the issue. The issue was that they had removed themselves from the realm of God, from the realm of reality and light, and placed themselves in the realm of superficiality and darkness.

We cannot live in any degree of darkness and have true meaningful fellowship with God. God doesn't step into the darkness to fellowship with us we must step into the light where He lives to commune with Him there. Coming to God in openness and humility, through Jesus Christ, does just that (1 John 1:5-9). Being real is the gateway to intimacy with God.

Openness is also the basis of real relationship and fellowship with other people. If you are living in pretence and I am doing the same then the way we relate to each other will be nothing but a charade. It will be artificial and shallow.

As mentioned, I am the most relaxed and comfortable with the people who I have been the most vulnerable with. When there is mutual openness it makes for genuine relationship and deep, meaningful fellowship. The leadership teams that I have served on that have valued open living and mutual accountability have not only been the most rewarding but have also been the most effective and operated at a high degree of spiritual authority.

Being open with our friends does make us vulnerable. There have been times that I have been candid and open with brothers and regretted it, especially when it has not been mutual. On occasion, my openness with and accountability to my leadership has been misconstrued or even used against me. But then, Jesus was betrayed by one of His team, denied by a close friend, and let down by the rest of His friends in His time of greatest need. That doesn't take away from the freedom and authority that comes from being real.

Being in meaningful open relationships with others is also the basis for fruitfulness and growth. We were never created to be isolated islands or to live independently of others. All of nature is reliant on symbiotic relationships and cross pollination in order to thrive. In the same way we can only thrive in mutually interdependent relationships with others whether that be spiritually or in our family or business and professional life.

The way we relate to other people reflects how real our relationship with God is. If we claim to have an intimate and dynamic relationship with God but find it difficult to get along with the other people in our lives, then we are bluffing ourselves. The Bible is clear that we cannot claim to love God yet not get along with other people, or claim to love God whom we have not seen if we cannot even love our brothers and sisters who we see every day (1 John 4:19-21).

I am not suggesting that our relationship with people is equally as intimate as our relationship with God, but our relationship with God through Jesus must translate into better relationships with others, or else we are just pretending or playing games. When we have a life-changing encounter with Jesus, then that must transfer into us being able to relate better to others. The more like Christ we become the deeper our relationships with others should be. We cannot claim to have an intimate relationship with God while at the same time asserting that we have difficulties getting along with others. Being real with God enables us to be real with people.

It should be obvious that if we are going to rightly represent Jesus as 'the light of the world' then we ought to be living where He lives - in the light. Jesus said, 'While I am in the world, I am the light of the world' (John 9:5).

But He also said, 'You are the light of the world. A town built on a hill cannot be hidden' (Matthew 5:14). These two statements may seem contradictory but they are not. He is simply saying that we are to be Him to the world around us. In fact, He commissioned us with 'Peace to you! As the Father has sent Me, I am sending you' (John 20:21). We are sent to be Jesus to the world.

I heard of a young man who came to know Christ as His Lord and Saviour in a city in Mexico. He had stumbled into church in a drunken state and radically encountered God. He was taken into the church fellowship and loved and discipled through a period of rehabilitation and spiritual growth. After two years, he was serving as youth leader in the church and city-wide community.

He was invited to participate in a secular live television talk show that debated the youth problems of the city. On answering one of the questions he referred to Jesus as the only hope for the city and started sharing his testimony of conversion. He was cut short by the talk show host who interrupted with, 'I don't believe in this God stuff.' He then plucked a pen out of his pocket and, waving it around, continued: 'Do you see this pen? I believe in this pen because I can see this pen. I believe in this pen because I can feel this pen. Why don't you bring your God to me so that I can see Him? Bring Him so that I can feel Him?'

The young man bowed his head for a moment and looked up into the cameras with the reply, 'Sir you don't understand. I was notorious in this town. The people of this town know me. They know that I grew up on the streets of this town addicted to sniffing glue. Sir, they know that I was a drug addict and an alcoholic. They know that I ran with the gangs and did time in the youth penitentiary in this town for violent crime. And Sir, they also know that when Jesus came into my life I became a new person. Sir, if you want to see God, look at me! Sir, if you want to feel God, touch Me!'

I am not advocating that we should run into the streets and approach the first person we meet with 'Do you want to see God? Look at me.' Or tap someone on the shoulder the next time we are in the check-out line in the supermarket with 'Excuse me. Do you want to feel God? Then touch me!' But I am suggesting that this should be our attitude. We should live in such a way that when people see our lives they should be seeing Jesus. When they come into contact with our lives they should encounter Him.

Do not be deceived, God is not mocked; for whatever a man sows, that he will also reap. For he who sows to his flesh will of the flesh reap corruption, but he who sows to the Spirit will of the Spirit reap everlasting life. Galatians 6:7,8 (NKJV)

It is a simple principle of sowing and reaping. Openness – living in the light - is our protection against deception.

Walking 'in the flesh' is akin to walking in darkness and the deception of functioning independently from God. That will ultimately lead to disaster. The Bible clearly warns against the fallacies of pride and that pride precedes destruction and that an arrogant spirit comes before a fall (Proverbs 16:18). In the passage about the fall of Satan in the book of Isaiah Satan refers five times in the space of two verses that 'I will ascend to the heavens; I will raise my throne above the stars of God; I will sit enthroned; I will ascend above the clouds; I will make myself like the Most High' (Isaiah 14:13,14, emphasis added). He is then instantly expelled from heaven.

PrIde and selfIshness is the essence of sIn and the catalyst for deception. Independence is based in prIde.

Over the many years in ministry, including being involved as mediator in some awkward and painful situations, I have seen a predictable pattern emerge that I refer to as 'The Deception Spiral'. The downward spiral starts with a lack of openness that is based in pride and pretence. It manifests as super spirituality, secretiveness, a spirit of independence, and often discontentment. Discontentment was the initial manifestation of pride when Satan was not content with who God created him to be. Independence leads to a lack of submission and accountability, which is akin to rebellion. The person is reluctant to be answerable to anybody and spiritualises their actions. This person is then out from under godly authority and protection and is functioning in their own authority, which is no authority at all, leaving them vulnerable to enemy influence. They become unteachable and vulnerable to deception as a result. Disobedience to previously held convictions becomes easier and easier. The result is deception and spiritual barrenness.

On the other hand, openness, or living in the light is based in humility and being real. This is expressed in honesty, integrity, being naturally spiritual, mutually interdependent, and great contentment. This results in an attitude of submission to leadership providing spiritual protection and authority. It is a safe place. This person is open to truth, welcomes conviction, responds to fresh revelation, and grows spiritually. Living in obedience to God becomes as normal as breathing. The inevitable outcome is abundant spiritual life and fruitfulness.

How do we shift from the downward spiral of deception to the upward spiral of authentic life? By humility! By acknowledging our need of God and others and coming out into the open. It is humility that transitions us from confusion to clarity; from insubordination to submission; from resisting truth to embracing it and from merely existing to being fully alive.

oOo

Chapter 10
Trusting God

Trust in the LORD with all your heart and
lean not on your own understanding; in
all your ways submit to him, and he
will make your paths straight.
Proverbs 3:5,6

*Never be afraid to trust an unknown
future to a known God.*
Corrie ten Boom

It was late August 1974. Cecilia and I had just returned to Johannesburg after a two-month 'Summer of Service' in Amsterdam as the conclusion of our eight months with Youth with a Mission in Europe. We were preparing for our first mission assignment in Harare, Zimbabwe then still Salisbury, Rhodesia. Loren Cunningham, the leader of our School of Evangelism (SOE) and founder of YWAM had requested us to plan and lead a School of Evangelism in Rhodesia, in January 1975, on similar lines to the one we had just attended in Switzerland.

We were due to be taken to Salisbury by Rudy Lack, a veteran YWAMmer who had led the first SOE earlier in the year in Rhodesia. He had been trailblazing in South Central Africa with special focus on the Chinese construction workers building the Tanzania to Zambia (Tanzam) rail line. He would visit the construction sites and hand out gospels of John in the form of Mao Tse Tung's little red book. He was going to introduce us to a few people who had shown interest in the ministry of YWAM and then leave back to his home in Switzerland.

Two days before our departure I was contacted by Pastor Derick Stone, who I had never met before, and asked to pay him a visit on the Sunday afternoon after church. Derick had been part of the delegation of seventy South Africans at the YWAM International outreach during the Olympic Games in Munich, Germany in 1972 and was keen to see YWAM established in Southern Africa. He had heard of our assignment to Rhodesia and wanted to meet us and express his support. We exchanged a few pleasantries and then without too much ado he casually handed me the keys to a low mileage sparkling white 1968 Mercedes Benz 200 and blessed us for our upcoming pioneering effort. A widow had left the car in his care to pass on to missionaries. We were the fortunate recipients.

Just nine months prior to this Cecilia and I had sold our 1968 Toyota Corona to pay for our airfares to Switzerland to attend the SOE and God was replacing it with a 1968 Mercedes Benz even before we could ask or trust Him for another vehicle. (It probably still costs the equivalent of a medium-sized five-year-old car today for two airfares between South Africa and Europe).

We subsequently put over 100,000 miles on that vehicle travelling and ministering all over South Central Africa. From that day until the time of writing - a period of over forty years - we have never been without reliable transport that we could use with confidence and at short notice to take on any journey that our work required: a wonderful testimony to God's faithful provision over many years.

On the Monday, we sorted out the paperwork for the Mercedes Benz and set off in our own vehicle for our first pioneering project. The shining silver star of the Mercedes Benz emblem on the front of the gleaming white bonnet (hood) was a great source of encouragement and a constant reminder of God's provision and personal involvement in our lives. What a confirmation as we followed Rudy Lack, on the road north out of Johannesburg, on an exciting undertaking into the unknown.

Having left on our journey a few hours later than originally anticipated we missed the closing time at the Beitbridge border post by a few minutes and consequently spent the first night of our new adventure under the African sky (in a 'billion-star hotel') on the warm tarmac beside the car. At least we were the first in line for the border crossing at opening time the next morning.

In Salisbury we were to trust God for a venue, recruit students, invite speakers, and plan a field trip for a SOE to start in less than five months. We innocently got on with doing the possible and trusted God for the impossible. The School did start on 1 January 1975 with forty students from twelve nations as a testimony to the goodness and faithfulness of God.

Naïve Faith

As I reflect on our first pioneering assignment I realise how naïve we were and how God's amazing enabling grace and provision was at work. It was not our great faith at work but rather a 'gift of faith'. Loren Cunningham had asked us to pray about doing it, we felt that God said yes, and then we just got on with it.

Before people could tell us that it was impossible it had already been done. If I would be asked now, after decades in the ministry with many pioneering efforts under the belt and a lot more experience, to go to a country that I had never been to before and set up a training program within five months, where I needed to find a venue, recruit students and staff, and invite lecturers, I would probably hesitate, even with the modern means of communication and technology available to me now.

Why would I hesitate? Because I now better understand some of the implications of such a pioneering effort. I have climbed some of those mountains over the years and I know some of the implications and challenges involved. I now know how high some of those mountains are. I have become too clever and experienced for my own good. Oh! How I long for the uncluttered naïve faith again that just gets on with obeying God without hesitation.

Learning to Trust

It was now October 1974. Cecilia and I had only been in Rhodesia for a few months when we were invited to speak at a missions conference in Pietermaritzburg, South Africa – an ideal opportunity to recruit students for the School of Evangelism. I had diligently sought God by prayerfully considering the invitation and the timing implications of the travel. I had peace in my heart that we needed to embrace the opportunity and had a conviction that we needed to set off on the 1600km journey at the latest by midday on the Thursday afternoon to make it to the conference by Friday evening.

There was a problem though. On Thursday morning I had only $8 (Rhodesian) in cash and half a tank of petrol. My logic said that you don't set off on a long journey under those circumstances. We carefully packed the car and waited for the mail. (Some trust in God and some trust in the mail). The mail came but there was no miraculous provision. It was already midday. Cecilia was waiting patiently in the car and I was sitting at my desk in the YWAM office reflecting on Proverbs 3:5,6 and wrestling with God about the direction to leave and whether I had got it wrong or not.

I started saying the verses, which were two of my most favourite memory verses, as a deliberate means of encouraging myself:

Trust in the Lord - Lord I am trusting You as much as I know how to - with all your heart - I am trusting You by choice willingly and wilfully with all my heart - in all your ways acknowledge Him - Lord as best as I know how I am honouring You in all that I do - and He shall direct your paths – Lord I know that You will direct my paths. I trust you.

What do I do now? I felt the Holy Spirit prompt me to say the verses again. So as intentionally and succinctly as I knew how I quoted them again.

Trust in The Lord with all your heart and lean not to your own understanding! Although I had probably quoted those verses dozens of times previously I had never really seen or heard those words. That's exactly what I was doing – leaning to my own understanding. My mind said, 'you cannot take on a long journey without enough money for fuel' my heart was saying 'Trust God!'

I felt a surge of faith in my spirit to obey God and to trust Him for provision along the way. I joined Cecilia in the car outside. 'Has God provided?' she immediately asked. 'No' I responded, 'but we are going to trust God' and quickly explained what I had just experienced. We started the car and set off on our journey already an hour later than anticipated.

We had been reading about Mel Tari and the revival in Indonesia. At one stage, they experienced God supernaturally refuel their vehicle when they were stuck in a remote area without fuel. We thought we might experience the same but our fuel gauge seemed to drop quicker than ever. When I had an opportunity, I used the $8 I had to buy fuel. The rest was now up to God.

We planned to route our trip via the town of Gwelo to visit a ministry team in need of some encouragement. They had been going through a difficult patch, their supplies were dwindling and their vehicle was in the garage for repairs. The least we thought we could do was to swing by on the way to encourage them to keep on trusting God.

On arrival, they were in high spirits and were a source of great encouragement to us. They had seen some spiritual breakthroughs in their ministry at a local school and the coffee bar outreach that they were serving in. Their vehicle had been repaired at no cost and they had returned home to boxes of food placed at their front door anonymously.

After a time of rich fellowship and prayer together we started towards the car to depart on the rest of our journey. One of the team was a young man from Norway. He shyly walked alongside me and explained that he had received some money in the mail that we had brought from the city and wanted to bless us with the tithe. He asked if I was willing to receive the gift. Was I willing? I suppressed my exuberant excitement and humbly received the gift with much thanks. We could refuel the car and continue our journey.

In South Africa we saw further provision through our family and friends and could make it on time to the conference in Pietermaritzburg. At the missions conference two students were successfully recruited for the subsequent School of Evangelism.

The issue here is not how the provision came but the principle of trusting God rather than the circumstances. We learnt the lesson to follow the conviction of our hearts rather than to rely on our own insight or limited understanding. We established the principle early on not to base our faith or our obedience or our guidance on the circumstances in which we found ourselves but rather on the character of God and the principles and promises in the Word of God.

God has often reminded me of the 'tank of petrol' incident when I have been overwhelmed by the circumstances around me and taken my focus off obeying His directions and trusting Him. As I focused on the sometimes overwhelming odds and difficult circumstances my faith would dwindle and all but disappear. But as I took my eyes off the circumstances and fixed them on the nature and character of God, and on the principles and promises in the Word of God, and on His faithfulness in the past, faith would come. Fresh faith would be released in my heart. I realised that I did not need a lot of faith, I just needed a big God. My faith needed to be focussed on Him. The principle of trusting Him remains constant despite the circumstances in which we find ourselves.

Lean Not on Your Own Understanding!

Leaning not on your own understanding does not mean you kiss your brains goodbye and do foolish or unintelligent things and then expect God to bail you out. Trusting God or taking a step of faith is not a blind leap into nothing. To trust God is to have a firm belief in the authenticity of His character and the reliability of His word. To trust God is not to step into oblivion but rather to lean heavily into Him and to believe that He is who He says He is and will do what He says he will do. It is to believe that he is more reliable than the perceived reality around you. He is a firm foundation. It is only when you step away from God, in disobedience to Him, that you step into nothing.

What it does imply, though, is when you know what God's will is and your mind says it is not going to work out, then you trust God and not your mind. The will of God and the ways of God seldom compute or make sense to our finite minds.

Perfect Peace in a War Zone

The Old Testament prophet Isaiah declares a wonderful promise and principle: 'You will keep him in perfect peace, whose mind is stayed on You, because he trusts in You' (Isaiah 26:3).

The first time this principle came alive to us was during the 'bush war' in Rhodesia. Cecilia and I were serving on an Elim mission station on the Mozambique border when we were caught up in a 'contact' between insurgents and the local security forces. On the Sunday morning we had taken a small team to a nearby village to conduct the worship service. We had been there the previous Sunday and most of the village had attended. This Sunday was different. Only a few ladies and children were there to welcome us. We rang the church bell and waited. Only a half-dozen or so more people joined us. There was an eerie silence and an unusual lack of activity in the village. After a long wait we conducted a short service and made our way back to the mission station.

A short distance outside the village an elderly man flagged us down and asked if he could be dropped off at the police station near the mission. We discovered that the villagers were being held hostage in their huts by so-called 'freedom fighters' from across the border. They would often raid the villages to get supplies, intimidate the locals, and abduct the woman to carry their weapons inconspicuously concealed in baskets of grain. Our passenger had gone to report this.

When the helicopter gunships started circling the area we knew that the war had come to our doorstep. We could hear explosions and small arms fire. The unfortunate result of such a 'contact' was that innocent locals were often caught in the crossfire. Very soon the helicopters started evacuating wounded people to the clinic where we were stationed. I helped out of the helicopter a twelve-year-old boy who had been badly wounded by shrapnel from an explosion. A soldier handed me an empty vial of morphine with a clear instruction to tell the medical staff at the clinic that he had already been injected with it.

Amidst all this noise, havoc, death, and suffering around us we went through the motions of assisting where we could as if we had been in this situation many times before. We can both testify to experiencing an uncanny peace – in fact a perfect peace. It was a peace that we could not manufacture ourselves or just pretend to be having. It was as if someone else was having peace through us. We know who that someone is. He is The Prince of Peace! It is not a peace that you can self-generate or stir up with human effort or just choose to have even with the strongest will. It is a peace that is independent of circumstances and the turmoil in which you find yourself and comes from the Christ within living His life through you.

Perfect Peace and Medical Challenges.

In February 2011 Cecilia was diagnosed with breast cancer. I remember the moment when we received the news that the tests had shown that she had aggressive cancer and needed surgery within days. Instead of being gripped by panic or fear a supernatural peace settled over us again - the perfect peace of The Prince of Peace.

We immediately felt stirred in our hearts to do the possible and to trust God for the impossible. We were very grateful for medical science and the technological advancement, especially in cancer treatment. We decided to submit to medical intervention while at the same time to trust God as the healer. Cecilia's attitude was that she couldn't lose. If she went to heaven she would win and if she were healed she would win. She was determined to trust God whether He healed her or not. Through almost an entire year of three sets of surgery, months of chemotherapy, weeks of radiation therapy and dark and difficult moments we were sustained by the grace of God and the perfect peace of Christ that comes to those who trust Him. His grace truly was sufficient.

The Peace of God and Guidance.

We have learnt through the years to put a high premium on the 'peace of God' or the 'witness of the Holy Spirit' when it comes to guidance. When we feel or believe we should be doing something in obedience to God but experience a lack of peace we take that seriously. Let peace act as a referee or umpire. We have found in guidance that we can often get the timing or sequence of events wrong if we just presumptuously blunder along. We don't ignore a lack of peace.

I like what Paul the Apostle wrote to the church in Philippi in this regard. 'Don't worry about anything, but pray about everything. With thankful hearts offer up your prayers and requests to God. Then, because you belong to Christ Jesus, God will bless you with peace that no one can completely understand. And this peace will control the way you think and feel' (Philippians 4:6,7 CEV).

Most of the teaching that I have heard on divine guidance puts a lot of weight on the circumstances working out as confirmation of the guidance. Cecilia and I are personally not guided by circumstances, as they are seldom favourable to start off with. We prefer to trust God and His faithfulness rather than the circumstances in which we find ourselves. Besides, when we focus on the circumstances we are in, our small faith dissipates very quickly. In turn, when we concentrate our small faith on God and His character the little faith we have multiplies. It is not how big your faith is but rather how big your God is.

Although we never base our guidance and subsequent steps of obedience on circumstances we have learnt that provision and the working out of the circumstances follows trusting and obeying. Our way of 'acknowledging God in all our ways and trusting Him to direct our paths' is based on the following three simple principles of guidance.

First, a word from God, which can come in various ways. We don't put God in a box and dictate how He should speak to us. We are open to Him speaking to us in any way He chooses. Secondly, the Peace of the Holy Spirit. We never ignore a lack of peace especially with regards to timing or sequence. We let the peace of God act as a referee or umpire: 'And the peace of God, which transcends all understanding, will guard your hearts and your minds in Christ Jesus' (Philippians 4:7). And thirdly, wise counsel. We submit our ideas to one another and to others who honour God. Remember the 'Fear of God' is the beginning of wisdom. We don't even consider counsel from those who do not honour God.

The basic principle in guidance is that you need to have three things line up. In fact you only need two points to draw a straight line but the third is for a check or confirmation. We discount circumstances as our confirmation and use the 'wise man principle' as our check and balance. Apart from putting a high value on 'peace' we also submit what we believe to be the word of God to us for wise counsel from people who are more objective than we would be in the circumstances.

The Wise Man Principle

The wise King Solomon said, 'Where there is no counsel, the people fall; but in the multitude of counselors there is safety' (Proverbs 11:14 NKJV).

Allow me to explain the outworking of this principle. We are talking here about not basing our confirmation on whether the circumstances work out or not but on something weightier than that.

I base my decision on whether to submit our guidance to others on the effect that our subsequent actions will have. If it only affects the family, then we keep it in the family. To the degree that it goes beyond just the family we submit it to that extent.

For example, if I 'dream up' some 'good idea' my first line of submission is to Cecilia as my wife. Usually if I can get it past her then it might be of God and is worth pursuing. I have realised that although I carry the weight of responsibility for decisions affecting our family Cecilia has the greatest influence through her heightened perception and sensitivity to these matters. I have learnt that it behoves me to listen to her opinion and what she believes God might be saying to her. A classic example of this is how God prepared her for our move to London long before I even became aware of the possibility.

Doxa Deo London

Unbeknown to us Willie and Sarie Stewart, very dear friends who we had known since 1985, were catalysts in us ending up in London. Willie frequented London on business. On these entrepreneurial trips he came across many young South Africans. They were mostly graduates, on two-year working holiday visas, holding down menial jobs to pay off their student loans and seeking opportunities to build their careers. They worked on the underground rail network, in construction, and in department stores, including the renowned Harrods. They mostly lived in cheap crowded communes.

Willie had a burden for these young people to be pastored and looked after spiritually and shared his vision with Alan Platt, the senior visionary leader of the Doxa Deo church. The vision of the church was to see cities transformed by the glory of God (the 'doxa of Deo') to places where Christ reigns. There was already a goal to see the ministry expand from Pretoria into twelve strategic cities. There were also several Doxa Deo members already in London asking to be cared for pastorally. In Christian parlance, this is referred to as a 'Macedonian call' in reference to a God-given vision that re-directed the apostle Paul from Asia Minor to take the Gospel message to Europe for the first time (Acts 15:39—18:22).

In 2003, after being in Doxa Deo Pretoria for six and a half years, Alan Platt called me into his office. With a map of London sprawled over his desk, he asked me if Cecilia and I would consider establishing the first international Doxa Deo church in London. He regarded me as a pioneer and felt that because of our international experience and me being English-speaking, we could be ideal candidates. He did ask me to keep it under wraps, as he had not said anything to the rest of the team yet. This was just an initial conversation. He wanted me to give it some prayer and some thought before we made any announcements.

At that stage I had thought that my international involvement in ministry was over. Up until then I had had a good innings in the nations but was now confined to home base as an urban missionary. I did take solace from the fact that I was helping to pioneer the Doxa Deo campus in the inner city of Pretoria amongst the many refugees from Zambia, Rwanda, Burundi, the Democratic Republic of Congo, and other places. Those that I was investing in would hopefully go back to their respective nations some day and make a difference there.

As I prayed and considered the possibility of a new initiative again I became excited. I was reminded of the faithfulness of God through many pioneering endeavours over the years. Memories came flooding back to me of God doing the impossible as we did what we could. I experienced a fresh release of faith and grace for a new challenge – some may call it an apostolic anointing. I was again spoilt for the ordinary and wanted to trust God for more. I carried this excitement in my heart for about two weeks without sharing it with Cecilia. After all, Alan Platt had asked me to keep it under wraps.

I eventually did broach the subject with her over morning tea by asking her if she knew what the vision of Doxa Deo was. 'Yes I know! We want to go to twelve cities,' she replied confidently. Then she asked inquisitively 'Where are we going, just not somewhere in South Africa?', I was taken aback by that question and asked her to explain. She in turn encouraged me to first share what was on my heart.

I continued to tell her that Alan Platt had asked us to pray about leading a pioneer team to London. I watched for a reaction from her but she didn't flinch one bit. She then went on to explain to me that she had already known for six months that we were going to re-locate internationally. She didn't know specifically that it would be London, but God had told her to start lifting her roots and get ready for a move. She reminded me that she had been 'spring cleaning' the house, tidying cupboards, and trashing unnecessary stuff. That was her step of faith in response to the prompting of God and an indication of her lifting her roots.

At that stage we as a family of six where comfortably living together in suburbia and getting on with the rhythm of life. Such a move to London would radically change things. Cindy-Joy was due to get married. David, then 14 and still at school, would have to accompany us. John and Donovan would have to set up home on their own. Because of this radical impact on all the family we submitted the guidance of us going to London to the four of them. We felt that if any one of them had a hesitation about us going to London we would have to re-consider.

Cindy–Joy was the first to respond with a resounding 'yes', feeling that God was opening a great new opportunity for us and that we would be foolish not to take it. The boys similarly felt a witness in their hearts that this was what we should do. The ratification of that decision took many more months. As it was not just affecting us as a family but had far-reaching implications for the church it had to be approved by the Apostolic Empowerment Team of Doxa Deo.

After much research, as well as a reconnaissance visit to London in September 2003, it was realised that it was not financially feasible to church plant with an entire team from South Africa. In fact, our support couldn't be guaranteed from South Africa but would have to be raised in London. We decided to go in faith and to trust God. The word of God, the peace in our hearts, and the wise counsel of many far outweighed the financial circumstances.

On 1 April 2004 we officially started the planting of Doxa Deo in London with three committed families. They had already been tithing into a fund for the previous six months and committed to continue. From the outset, we could be housed and fed and during the first year we could send £1,000 per month to South Africa as our 'first fruit'. This was a wonderful conformation from God that we were indeed in His will and that we could trust Him 'to make our paths straight'.

Wider Submission

In 1994 I had a dream of mobilising 2,000 missionaries from South Africa by the year 2000. I was then still the Southern Africa director of YWAM. Because this had implications beyond just YWAM I submitted the idea to my friends Francois Vosloo the national director of Operation Mobilisation (OM); Willie Crew the director of the World Mission Centre (WMC); and Murray Louw the director of the South African Action for World Evangelism (SAAWE). Not surprisingly they all had a similar vision to mobilise South Africans into missions. The upshot was a series of 'Love Southern Africa' mission conferences and collaborative efforts to mobilize South Africans into missions.

In May 1995 we attended the Global Consultation of World Evangelisation (GCOWE) hosted by the AD2000 and Beyond Movement in the beautiful Torch Center, home of the Korean Center for World Mission, in Seoul Korea. We gathered together with almost 4,000 delegates from 186 countries to consult on a collective vision for missions leading up to the year 2000 and beyond. Apart from the plenary sessions, the conference was divided into different tracks such as Prayer, Media, Youth, Literature etc. For two days, we in the 'missions track' consulted together under the leadership of George Verwer from OM and Pari Rickhard from YWAM on a vision for missions by the year 2000 and beyond. Each track had to report back to the conference in the final plenary session. Verwer and Rickhard reported that the vision for the missions' track was to mobilise 200,000 new missionaries by the year 2000. This seemed like a daunting task and a massive faith proclamation; as it would mean doubling the mission force in the world in just five years.

On the very next day the Korean Student Movement hosted the conference at a rally in the Seoul Olympic Stadium. I have a vivid memory of us 4,000 delegates being welcomed as we walked down the 100-metre athletic track of a stadium packed almost to its 100,000 capacity to rapturous applause and flag waving. I closed my eyes for a moment and imagined being one of the Olympians being cheered on as I ran the sprint.

The students had gathered for two reasons: to pray for missions and to be commissioned into the mission field. We participated in the

Korean-style prayer meeting where everyone in the stadium prayed in unison and at full volume for the same subject. A signal would be given over the public-address system and the stadium would fall silent. The next prayer subject would be announced and the multitude would break out in enthusiastic united prayer again. This went on for some time.

The most poignant moment for me was the commissioning of 75,000 students into the mission field. I witnessed as they stood with their right hands raised pledging their commitment to join the worldwide task of penetrating the unreached peoples with the Gospel after graduating. They covenanted that if North Korea should open to South Korea they would suspend their studies with immediate effect, and first go to North Korea to plant a church before resuming their studies.

The day before we had dared to declare that we were going to trust God to mobilise 200,000 new missionaries in the next five years. Here we were witness to 75,000 of them already making that commitment. What a thrill and an amazing encouragement. We also learned that one congregation, the Onnuri Presbyterian Church in Seoul, committed to sending 2,000 members of its 8,000-member church to the mission field by the year 2000 and asked their church members for a lifetime commitment to pray daily for their missionaries and world evangelization.

Trusting God in Impossible Situations

Faith can have an 'in case' in it.

Having a contingency plan when trusting God in impossible situations does not mean you don't have faith; it just means you don't know the outcome for sure. When David confronted the Philistine giant, Goliath, with his modest little sling he collected five stones. Why five stones and not just one? In case! In case what? In case he missed the first time or in case Goliath had some brothers. David was not being pretentious. He was using what was familiar to him and doing what he could with what he had. He did the possible and trusted God for the impossible. He submitted what he could do to God and trusted Him for the outcome.

Faith can have a 'maybe' in it.

In about 1050 BC a massive Philistine army was assailing King Saul and a band of 600 unarmed fearful men who were hiding in caves, wells, and thorn bushes. The enemy had thousands of chariots, thousands of horsemen, and an uncountable number of infantry soldiers. It was an impossible situation. During this impasse Jonathan says to his young armour-bearer, 'Come, let us go over to the garrison of these uncircumcised; it may be that the LORD will work for us. For nothing restrains the LORD from saving by many or by few' (1 Samuel 14:6 NKJV). They trigger the battle and God brings chaos and confusion amongst the enemy army, so much so that it destroys itself- all because two young men were willing to trust God against all the odds.

Faith does not compromise.

In the Old Testament book of Daniel, chapter three, there is a story of three Hebrew boys who were confronted with execution if they did not bow and worship King Nebuchadnezzar's idol. A furnace was being heated up seven times hotter than usual and they were going to be tossed into it if they did not comply. This is what they reply to the king: 'The God we worship can save us from you and your flaming furnace. But even if he doesn't, we still won't worship your gods and the gold statue you have set up' (Daniel 3:17,18 CEV). Because of not compromising and worshipping the idol they get thrown into the fiery furnace. During the fierce flames they experience perfect peace and fellowship with Jesus and come out unscathed.

I have had my fair share of enemy armies to contend with, giants to slay, and fiery furnace incidents to confront - and so have you. And there will no doubt be more challenges in the future. The question is: Are we willing to trust God against all odds and despite not having hundred percent assurance of the outcome?

Trusting God Always

Trust in Him at all times, you people; pour out your heart before Him; God is a refuge for us. Psalm 62:8 (NKJV).

Trusting God at all times simply means always. We trust God when things go well and when they don't. We trust Him when we are on the mountain-top of glory and victory and we trust God when we are in the valley of despair. We trust Him when we know what is going on and we trust Him when we don't. We trust Him when we have complete clarity and we trust Him when we don't understand. We trust Him when He provides our needs and we trust Him when He seemingly doesn't. We trust Him when He answers our prayers in the way we expect and we trust Him when He answers in a different way. We trust God when He says yes and we trust Him equally when He says no. We trust Him because He is trustworthy!

In April 2001 Cecilia went to hospital for what was to be a routine hysterectomy. She ended up staying for seven days and fighting for her life. It is in circumstances like these that I am grateful that we have learnt to trust God. I wonder what people do who don't have that anchor. I became very anxious when the one-hour procedure became three hours. The operation was much more complicated than the surgeon had anticipated. Cecilia had a frozen pelvis and her womb was cemented to her intestines. Extra specialist surgical help had to be called in. Her heart showed irregularities and she subsequently needed eight units of blood to replace the blood loss. I remember being taken aback by the complications and realized that I needed to lean into God and trust Him to bring us through. I couldn't fathom why the medical profession had been caught off-guard. I felt hopeless and helpless as I visited Cecilia in ICU over the next few days. It was hard to see her struggling like that. I was just hanging in there. All I knew to do was to trust God. And He came through for us. I am very grateful that Cecilia was in an excellent private hospital where she could get the professional care she needed and that we had medical aid to cover the costs.

Trusting God, and particularly Proverbs 3:5,6 has proved not just to be a 'hobby horse' of mine but has become our lifestyle as a family. I am trusting God to clearly 'direct my paths' for the rest of my life.

oOo

Chapter 11
God's Faithful Provision

For the Lord is good and his love endures forever;
his faithfulness continues through all generations.
Psalm 100:5

Where God guides, He provides.
Where He leads, He feeds.
If it is God's will it is God's bill.

These might sound like glib sayings or empty clichés but we now have more than four decades of testimony to God's faithful guidance and provision. In fact, these years are nothing short of a financial and material miracle and a huge encouragement for us to trust God for His sustained provision into the future. We have no reason to doubt that He will continue to adequately take care of us.

If you had to ask Cecilia to summarise, in just a few words, her experience of God during our life and ministry thus far, she would unhesitatingly say: 'God is faithful'. Our most favourite hymn is Great is Thy Faithfulness.

After our 'point of no return' in 1975 and commitment to do whatever God wanted us to do, He has always been faithful to guide us and to provide for us. Every time we have had to make a major shift geographically or in leadership responsibility, His direction has always been very clear. Often when those transition times came there was more than one option for us to consider. This required us to carefully reflect on what we believed the next step was and not to presume on the will of God.

We have also learnt, however, that God never gives you so much guidance that you don't need faith. He is faithful to make His plans clear to you through an objective personal word to you; the peace in your heart acting as a referee; and the independent wise counsel of others. But you still have to take your own step of faith in obedience to Him by trusting His character and His Word.

Similarly, as our needs increased with extensive travel, responsibilities, and a growing family, God's provision increased correspondingly. He is Jehovah Jireh, our provider.

During these forty-four years in full-time ministry we roughly spent the first twenty-five years in missions with YWAM, living in Southern Africa but travelling extensively to the nations. During the subsequent years we have been in local church ministry of which sixteen years were with Doxa Deo both in Pretoria and in London, and the rest of the time has now been with Restore Community Church in Loughton, London.

Throughout our time in missions we had no guaranteed income yet saw our needs met through the generosity of friends and family and God's miraculous provision. During the time of ministry in the local church we have had a monthly salary but continue to trust God for additional provision to meet our needs and do the things we believe He has called us to do.

For the first ten years of our ministry we did not solicit any support or tell anyone of our financial needs unless we were specifically asked. We were always very careful not to just glibly say 'we live by faith' as that could be wrongly construed to mean that 'we have God and we don't need you'. We knew that we were interdependent on others and needed them. We tried to be as honest and open as possible while still communicating our total dependence on God and our desire to ultimately do His bidding.

When the Israelites were in the wilderness for forty years God sustained them with the miraculous provision of fresh manna everyday but when they crossed the Jordan River into the Promised Land they had to fend for themselves and live off the land. There are two key principles of God's provision that converge for us as we continue to 'live by faith'. The first is 'living off the land' and the second is 'manna provision'. We trust God for both.

Living off the land implies 'working the land'. A harvest does not happen automatically. It takes the investment of time and energy. It involves ploughing, planting, watering, weeding, cultivating, pruning, then ultimately harvesting and enjoying the fruit of your labour. That means hard work. In the ministry, it is the same. There is no reward for laziness and irresponsibility. God rewards diligence and faithfulness.

Manna provision implies the miraculous. We have always been dependent on God's additional miraculous provision to supplement our regular income to do the things He wants us to do. We have seen manna provision in terms of vehicles, housing, and extensive travel. We have always sought to do the possible and trust God for the impossible.

A classic example of God's miraculous provision was when I got my Private Pilot's licence (PPL) in February 1980. At that stage we were leading the work of YWAM in Namibia and had workers deployed as teachers and nurses in remote areas in that vast nation. It would take a full day's drive, and sometimes longer, to reach some of these areas in a rugged four-wheeled-drive vehicle, whereas some of these destinations could be reached within a few hours in a light aircraft. I would often charter a flight for a day to make some of these pastoral visits. The pilots would encourage me that if I was going to do this kind of work in Namibia I needed to learn to fly. I was convinced!

A PPL required passing a medical, some theoretical exams, a minimum of forty hours of flight instruction, and a practical flight test. This would all come at considerable expense, none of which could come out of our personal household budget. The miracle came through a young graduate, Pam Hackett, who felt to give her first ever pay packet towards my PPL. It covered sixty percent of the cost. Thanks, Pam! The other forty percent was covered by a grant from the Department of Civil Aviation that was encouraging people to take up flying – if that is not another bit of amazing manna provision then I don't know what is. This helped me to get my licence within three months without being concerned where the money would come from.

Basic Needs

But more than anything else, put God's work first and do what he wants then the other things will be yours as well (Matthew 6:33 CEV).

God has encouraged me on numerous occasions through the years with the conviction that if I take care of His house, He will take care of mine. If I attend to His business, He will attend to mine.

In the Gospel of Matthew, chapter six, we learn that if we prioritise God and walk in His ways then our basic needs will be met. The context of the passage indicates that our basic needs are food, drink, and clothing. We have taken the liberty through the years to add transport or travel to that list and to trust God for His provision in that regard as well.

Years before we owned our own home we would proportionately spend large amounts of money annually on international and local travel. At times, I would be questioned about the wisdom of that. Would that money not be more prudently invested in a mortgage? My reply was always that I didn't have a pot of money at the beginning of the year to decide what to do with and if I hadn't travelled at all that year I wouldn't have had that money in surplus to decide what to do with. God provided for what He wanted us to do. Over many years of crisscrossing the globe and ministering in many nations, some of them multiple times, God has faithfully provided.

Housing

At the time when I was transitioning from the National Director to the Southern Africa Director of YWAM we needed to re-locate into the Johannesburg area to be close to the regional office. Over a period of months as I travelled into the city I would stretch my hand over the southern suburbs and ask God to direct us to the right rental property. One day I got a call from a pastor friend who did some teaching in YWAM schools from time to time. He wanted to talk to me about their house. I presumed that his house was available to rent.

I duly met with Cedric and Ingrid Coates in their spacious home, which they had named 'Charis', in the leafy suburb of Albemarle. They told me that they had been committed for years to sow their house into the Kingdom of God and felt more recently to offer it to Cecilia and me. They immediately qualified it by saying that they could not give us the house outright but that they wanted to make it available to us for the outstanding bond. That startled me, as purchasing a house had never been on our radar. Cedric handed me the mortgage documents and suggested that I pray about it, consult with whomever I needed to, and then speak to the building society that held the bond to see if they would be willing to help me.

On reporting back to Cecilia, she was just as taken aback as I had been. Purchasing a house seemed very daunting to us and completely outside our frame of mind and financial capability. That evening we saw the new Volkswagen Syncro 4x4 being advertised on television for the same price as 'Charis' was being offered to us. Cecilia's response was that we had trusted God for a VW Combi before - in fact we owned one at the time – so we immediately had faith to trust God for the house.

On doing some research we realised that the house was being offered to us at sixty-five percent of the municipal valuation and at substantially less than the replacement value. I consulted with my leadership; both my and Cecilia's parents; and our support team. They all agreed that this was God's provision for us and that we should pursue the possibility of a purchase.

One of the agents at the building society was initially very sceptical and suspicious that someone would want to sell a house for the outstanding mortgage when the market value was substantially higher. She told me that she did not believe that there were such people on earth. I was very open and candid when I spoke with the manager of the building society. I told him that I did not have any money for a deposit or for administration and transfer costs and that I could not produce pay slips to show any guaranteed income. To cut a long story short, they offered us a hundred and five percent loan on the basis that the property was worth substantially more than we needed to borrow. The additional money was to cover the administration and legal fees. Our monthly repayment on the mortgage ended up being significantly less than the monthly rent on a similar property. The house was a great blessing to us as a family of six. We are grateful for God's faithful provision and indebted to the Coates family for their amazing generosity.

After owning 'Charis' for eight years we were able to sell it for 2.7 times the initial purchase price and reinvest the money in a property in Pretoria, when we joined the Doxa

Deo team there. On relocating to London another seven years later we were, in turn, able to sell that house for 2.4 times what we paid for it and use the equity to buy a three-bedroom town house, mortgage free, for our sons John and Donovan to move into. I share all this with the utmost gratitude and as a testimony to God's faithful provision. It all started with the humble obedience and generosity of a couple that was also in the ministry. We are hugely appreciative of and indebted to them.

Housing in London

One of the major financial challenges in relocating to London was the cost of housing, although we have always asserted that God is not daunted by the value of the currency or the prevailing economic climate in which we find ourselves.

We initially rented a town house for £1,000 per month, which quickly grew to £1,200. At that stage I was driving a very reliable ten-year-old Toyota Camry that had been gifted to me by a local minister, worth about £600. When colleagues from South Africa visited, they commented on the fact that in South African Rand terms I was probably earning more than any of them - albeit my salary being confidential. My response was that, equally so, I was living in the smallest house and driving the oldest car. And besides I was paying the equivalent of two cars for my monthly housing. I wondered what percentage of their cars they were paying on housing.

When we were planning our move to London our long-standing entrepreneur friend, Willie Stewart, told me that he had come up with the idea of creating a 'floating tithe'. He was going to sell a property in Spain and create a fund with ten percent of the money to help people, like us in the ministry, with an indefinite, interest free loan to get on the property ladder. He offered us his assistance. I was intrigued by the idea but filed it in the back of my mind as I have had many offers from people who were going to make money and then help support people in missions that never materialised.

Within fifteen months of being in the UK, Willie Stewart called me to say that they had sold the house in Spain and that we could start looking for a house to buy. In fact, he and his wife were going to be in

London within the next few months and they would help us look for one. That all materialised and within six months we had moved into our own town house, purchased with the help of a substantial deposit from our friends. The deposit helped to secure the mortgage, as we had no credit history in the UK. Our monthly mortgage repayment was a lot less than we had been paying on monthly rent but we decided that it would benefit us in the long term to keep paying at the same level. It has made a massive difference over a twelve-year period. Good stewardship pays off!

Currently we only owe thirty-five percent of the market value of the property. This is another massive testimony to God's faithful provision; the generosity of His people and a validation of His principles of stewardship. I am very aware that property markets are volatile and can change at any time affecting our existing equity but our confidence and trust continues to be in God and not in the economy.

The Bigger Picture

God's thoughts are always far above our thoughts and His ways above ours. He always sees the bigger picture. In 1980 I was involved in my first daunting challenge of buying a property to serve as a training centre for YWAM Namibia. As I share some of that history don't think in terms of the currency values or exchange rates but rather on the incredible faithful provision of God in that context.

YWAM had been sending outreach teams to Namibia since 1978 and had established a mission house in the capital, Windhoek, led by Edmund and Marieta Pohl. Cecilia and I went to Namibia in 1980, initially for three months, and ended up staying for four years. We were there during the transition years from South West Africa to Namibia – some of the best years of our life.

In January 1980, we took a group of about twenty young people from South Africa to pioneer a Discipleship Training School (DTS) in Namibia. We spent the first month in a campsite in Okahandja, about seventy kilometres north of the capital Windhoek, while negotiating to buy a property on the outskirts of the capital to house the DTS.

In March that same year Ian Muir and I took what we saw as a major step of faith in signing the documents to purchase a large house, on about a hectare of land, for R110,000. We made R30,000 on the sale of the original house in the city, which meant we still had a loan of R80,000 to service. This seemed like a massive challenge at the time. The base proved to be a great blessing and served YWAM well as a training centre for many years.

After Namibia gained independence in March 1990 many embassies established themselves in the city and large-scale development took place around the YWAM property. The property was sold to a developer in 1995 for R2.3 million. The base was relocated to what used to be an agricultural college, with all the relevant accommodation and training facilities, on 910 hectares of farmland, just ten kilometres outside the city, for the purchase price of R1.45 Million. At the time of writing there are negotiations underway to sell a small portion of the farm on the outskirts of the city to a housing developer for in excess of R10 million. Whether that ever materialises or not I marvel at God's faithful provision and multiplication in response to our small steps of faith and obedience.

Family Sabbatical

In 1994, unbeknown to us, YWAM Southern Africa had a fund-raising initiative called Project Honour to thank us for twenty-one years of service in the mission. I was encouraged to take a year's sabbatical but we decided to settle for a four-month family break in the USA. The financial gift was sufficient to cover half the return airfares for our family of six from Johannesburg to New York. God faithfully provided all our expenses through the generosity of family and friends, including a loan to buy a vehicle and then sell it again to repay the loan at the end of the holiday.

We arrived in New York on 1 May and landed back in Johannesburg on 1 September after having travelled through twenty-two states. We rented a van in New York and drove to friends in Richmond, Virginia where we purchased a six-seater Plymouth Voyager for $3,000. We subsequently sold it for $3,300 after four months and 11,400 miles (19,000 kilometres). The profit covered our insurance for that period. While in West Virginia we, as a family, spent a few memorable nights on the Mercy Ship the M/V Anastasis in Norfolk. I had only been on the ship in Dakar Senegal three months previously.

We made many memories, had an unforgettable time as a family and were blessed out of our socks with God's extravagant blessing and protection, and the generosity of His people. We were overwhelmed by His grace and goodness and timely provision throughout that time. For instance, friends of ours from South Africa had gifted us with a week's timeshare at the Orlando International Resort – Disney World and Universal Studios – in Florida. The manager of the resort offered us an additional five days for a nominal fee of the levy as the unit we were using would be unoccupied for those days. What a blessing.

Although we were on a sabbatical I did have the opportunity to minister from time to time. While teaching for a few days at the YWAM DTS in Tyler, Texas a friend offered us their holiday cabin in the Rocky Mountains in Colorado, for two weeks, while they went on a trip to Russia. I envisaged a one-roomed log hut with a wood burning stove for cooking and meagre facilities, like you see in cowboy movies. Instead it was a spacious, multistoried mansion kitted out with satellite television, a hot tub, quad bikes, and snow mobiles for the winter. On returning from Russia, Cecilia asked our friend how they justified such an extravagant place just for their holidays. His reply was 'Mam, when we work, we work hard. When we play, we play well.'

We ended up staying in Cimarron in the Rocky Mountains at 8,500ft for a month, firstly at High Park Ranch the YWAM base, then at El Rancho-Chateau de Paris for two weeks and lastly in another friend's three-storey log house called Silver Jack. It was a memorable time with snow- clad mountain peaks towering above us at over 13,000ft, trout fishing every other day, and lots of hiking and quad biking in the forests.

One poignant memory that stands out to me of our time in Colorado was God's protection from a serious accident. As we neared our destination after a seven-hour journey from New Mexico, negotiating the narrow mountain passes, a large 4X4 truck came skidding around a blind corner at speed, narrowly missing us and rolling over the embankment just behind us. We could assist the father and two children out of the wreckage. Fortunately, they had no serious injuries. My journal entry for that day reads 'It was as if angels buffered our van. Reminded that as we left Stonewall at 10 am this morning David (then six) prayed specifically that God would protect us from accidents'. He did!

We set off on our holiday each with a suitcase, some of them only medium-sized, and a small bit of hand luggage. We returned with twelve large bags (two each) and hand luggage packed to the hilt. You can just imagine us manhandling that mountain of stuff at the airports. Nonetheless, a wonderful end to an exceptional family break with extraordinary memories that continue to be cherished.

Provision for Family

I have been astounded at God's faithful provision for us as a family through the years. As the family grew and our financial needs increased, God provided accordingly. Although we never lived in the lap of extravagant luxury, all our needs were adequately provided for. Thanks be to God! He is much more concerned for and committed to my family than I can ever be.

By God's grace we could successfully navigate the financial challenges of life without getting into financial difficulties or incurring major debts. All our children are adults today and happily live within their means without any debilitating liabilities to contend with. They never had the excessive extras in material things but their needs were always adequately provided for.

Both Cindy-Joy and Donovan were able to self-fund their commercial degrees (B.Com), through the University of South Africa (UNISA), while working full time and studying part time. Cindy went on to complete her teacher training at the University of Pretoria while Donovan completed a Masters in Business Administration with Regent University in the USA. John completed his Bachelor of Theology, also through UNISA, while serving as the worship leader at the church in London.

As David was finishing his A levels in the UK he was offered places at three universities to study Sports Conditioning and Coaching Science. The fees for foreign students varied from £6,500 to £13,500. We considered him taking an extended 'gap year' for three years as he would be a British Citizen by then and only have to pay £3,000 a year. However, based on David's swimming performance, the University of West England invited him to join their Modern Pentathlon Academy at the Hartpury campus in Gloucestershire. Although the school fees were £8,500 a year excluding accommodation they offered him a Principal's bursary of £2,000. In addition, he got a private scholarship for £3,000. As a family we felt that was enough indication of God's obvious provision and decided to trust Him for the rest. With extra jobs on campus providing accommodation David was able complete his four years of university training debt free as another testimony of God's faithful provision.

Together We Can Do More

In 2012 God started speaking to us as the International Leadership of the Doxa Deo group of churches that the vision of city transformation was not only for us. Alan Platt, the senior leader of the church, had a clear impression that we needed to move from being a 'branded house' to a 'house of brands' and challenged us to be on the lookout for strategic partnerships that God might want us to form. The Kingdom of God was much bigger than just us.

At that stage I was leading the Doxa Deo congregation in Loughton – meeting in Roding Valley School. A friend of mine, Ian King, was leading the Restore Community Church in Loughton – meeting in Davenant Foundation School just two miles away. Ian and I had been in fellowship over several years having been introduced to one another by common missionary friends, Toby and Aukje Brouwer, who were pioneering a ministry in Zambia. During 2012 we had a lot more contact as part of Churches Together in Loughton. We had already held a combined service and were considering joint services over Christmas and Easter.

The vision of Doxa Deo is 'City Transformation' and Restore's is 'Community Restoration'. Similar, just different terminology. In mid-September 2012, Ian King and I discussed partnering together and making our two congregations one. Days later my entire leadership team endorsed the idea of us embarking on a journey and the next day the Restore eldership were guided to a passage in Ezekiel 37 where the two sticks representing the two houses of Israel became one stick, representing one nation under God. We were all comfortable with investigating the possibility of joining resources to do more together.

The big questions such as leadership structure, legal responsibility, and how our salaries would be paid were resolved in literally a few minutes of frank discussion. The rest of the discussions meshing the two congregations together went smoothly. We fitted like hand in glove. God was obviously in it. On 16 December 2012 we had a joining service, presided over by Alan Platt, where Ian King and I symbolically laid down our individual staffs and picked them up as one, representing our togetherness and unity.

At the time of writing it has already been five years into the journey. It has been a win-win situation all round, and another testimony to the faithful provision and guidance of a trustworthy God.

Responsibility

Although God is abundantly faithful and trustworthy, we cannot live irresponsibly and think we can avoid the consequences. God is not a respecter of persons in that He randomly blesses some and not others. God does respect the principles He has given for us to live by and honours those who honour Him and who walk in His ways. The Bible has over 2000 verses related to money, more than any other single subject. This ought to say something to us.

In the next chapter we will investigate some of the guidelines for living in financial freedom as we yield to our heavenly Father. Jesus said 'No one can serve two masters. Either you will hate the one and love the other, or you will be devoted to the one and despise the other. You cannot serve both God and money' (Matthew 6:24).

oOo

Chapter 12
Living by Faith Financially

Look at the birds of the air;
they do not sow or reap or store away in barns,
and yet your heavenly Father feeds them.
Are you not much more valuable than they?
Matthew 6:26

But seek first the Kingdom of God and His
righteousness, and all these things
will be given to you as well.
Matthew 6:33

God our heavenly Father is the original owner of everything and that includes all that we have. There is nothing that we have, including the breath that we breathe, that did not originate from Him in the first place. God is so generous and kind, though. He entrusts life and possessions to us that we can use to bless others. Managing his gifts well and offering them back to Him as an act of worship, honours Him as the source of all we have

How we handle money, whether we have a lot or a little, is a clear indication of our relationship with God. It takes faith to handle finances responsibly and diligently. Everyone can 'live by faith' whether they are wealthy or financially challenged. By heeding biblical principles of faith and finances we can avoid the pitfalls that lead to anxiety and financial lack. The motives underpinning financial principles in God's Kingdom are quite different from the current world system. The acts of sowing and reaping, buying and selling, giving and receiving are common to both. The one system is guided by integrity, generosity, stewardship, and trusting God while the other is driven by fear of the future, greed, selfishness, materialism, and a confidence that mankind can fend for itself.

Seek First the Kingdom of God

Put God first! If Jesus is the Lord of your life, then He is Lord over your finances; you are only a manager or steward of them. Cecilia and I generally ask the question 'Is it the will of God?' before making a big purchase, spending large sums of money or making a long-term commitment financially. This is especially true if it involves future income that is not guaranteed. Spending presumptuously can get you into a lot of trouble. If it is God's will then you can confidently trust Him for His provision. If it is your own idea, then you pay the bill. If it is God's will then it is His bill. It is only expensive to live if you are selfish and greedy and living for yourself. It is only expensive to travel if you are running away from God. Then you pay – in more ways than only financially.

We divide our budget simply between the categories of Obligations, Needs, and Wants. Our projected income is then prayerfully divided into these priorities. Any major financial transaction outside the norm or unexpected financial need that crops up is carefully and prayerfully considered to make sure we are in the will of God and not making rash decisions. Examples of these include the purchase of a house or car, major travel expense outside of budget, holiday plans, and responding to appeals to invest in a charitable cause.

Walking Righteously

Because we are totally dependent on God for our guidance and provision it also behoves us to constantly walk in a right relationship with Him and to keep our consciences clear. God has the uncanny knack of using financial constraints to get our attention either to teach us a lesson, to grow our character, or to deepen our trust in Him. It is also an ideal opportunity to pause and confirm the direction of our lives. Moving ahead with a conviction that our lives are on track engenders faith.

I was once in a meeting in Europe where an offering was being taken for a few individuals who did not have all their finances to join us on an outreach. The names were written on the white board with the corresponding amounts that each still needed. We were encouraged to pray and ask God if we should participate in the giving and how much. I felt convicted to give an amount that represented all the spare money that Cecilia and I had for contingency expenses for the next few months. I checked with her and she confirmed that we could be generous to that extent. I looked up the list to find the amount we had in mind and then across to the name. When I saw the name my reaction was 'God anybody but him'. I realised I had a problem. I had to sort my heart attitude out and be reconciled with him and then give the money anonymously. Over the next three months Cecilia and I were sorely tested in our attitudes and generosity when we often witnessed this individual splurging on luxuries when we didn't have a dime to even buy an ice cream.

There are often temptations to compromise financially. If we are going to trust God financially we must walk in integrity in this area. It is not only a matter of us trusting God but of Him being able to trust us.

In the story that I related in Chapter 11 of the purchase of the Albemarle property in Johannesburg, a challenge arose. When it came to the final signing of the legal documents the attorney informed me that there was a fifteen percent gift tax due on fifty percent of the difference between the purchase price and the municipal valuation. This was a considerable amount of money. If I wasn't willing to sign we could cancel the deal and start the paper work over with a different purchase price, that I could come to an 'arrangement' on with the owner. This would avoid paying the tax but would complicate matters substantially and delay the process. I decided to go ahead and sign the documents and to trust God to pay the gift tax. Over the next few months I inexplicably received two cheques from the attorneys refunding most of their fees, which more than covered the gift tax.

All These Other Things

The context of Matthew 6 is that if we put God first and walk circumspectly before Him that He will provide our basic needs of food, drink, and clothing. Cecilia and I have learnt to take that slightly out of context and to trust God for travel expenses as a basic need as well. Part of what God has called us to do involves a lot of travel.

Although we have never lived in opulence and luxury we can testify to the fact that we as a family have never lacked anything. We have never had to miss a meal except by choice; have always had good clothes to wear and a roof over our heads; had our medical needs and expenses paid for; always had a reliable family car or cars; and never got into debt travelling in obedience to God.

Loving God Rather Than Things

Materialism is not having things it is when the things have us. The Bible does not say that money is the root of all evil but rather that the love of money is the root of all evil. Money is amoral – it is neither good nor evil – it is our attitude to and relationship with money that becomes the issue. We are to love God and others and to use things. It is when we confuse God's ways and start using people and even 'using' God because of our love for money and things that we become enslaved to material stuff.

The very first time I encountered this as an issue was when I decided not to return to my civil engineering training and career but to, at least initially, serve in missions for a few more years. Because I had studied through a Public Service Commission bursary I either had to work for the Commission for the equivalent years of my studies or pay back the money in full. Cecilia and I decided to do the possible and trust God for the impossible. The only thing we knew to do was to try and sell some of our possessions, realising that there was not a great market for our things. We mostly owned second-hand furniture that I had meticulously restored because of wanting to stay out of debt. It had more nostalgic value than monetary value and was definitely not nearly as valuable to anybody as what we needed.

I remember telling God that I was willing to let go of all our worldly possessions but would like to keep the high fidelity (Hi-Fi) stereo sound system. I realised immediately that I had a problem. I had become sentimentally attached to the amplifier of the system because I had built it from a kit. I spent many hours methodically soldering every tiny transistor, resistor, capacitor, and other electronic components onto a variety of circuit boards. I remember the moment of elation when everything was plugged in, the switch turned on, and it worked. Nothing exploded in my face. I tried to justify holding onto it and using it in ministry but realised very quickly that I needed to let it go. I was in bondage to it. It was in my heart and not just in storage somewhere.

Needless to say, we did sell a few of our things, the Hi-Fi sound system being the first to go, and within a few days saw the full provision of the money we needed to meet our obligation to the Public Service Commission. That 'exercise' not only taught us to hold onto things lightly but served as a massive confirmation that we were doing the right thing by staying involved in missions.

Generosity

Each time we gratefully give a tithe or an offering we are making a powerful statement of faith and exemplifying the character of God. Our gifts become acts of gratitude and worship that break the spirits of fear and greed that are so common in this generation. Generosity was customary in biblical times even before the Ten Commandments but the setting aside of the first tenth of the harvest or increase of livestock (called the tithe) to honour God and support the priesthood became part of Old Testament law (Leviticus 27:33,31). Jesus didn't come to set aside this law but to give us a higher one – the law of love. Our generosity is thus not a legalistic religious ritual but motivated by our love for God and others.

Cecilia and I resolved very early on in our mission career that the 'first fruit' of our income or the tithe, if you will, belongs to God and doesn't need to be negotiated every month. We decided that if we were going to depend on God for our financial security then we couldn't afford not to be generous. We discovered in any case that if we held back on the 'first fruit' or tithe we never got to use it anyway. It was always devoured in some way or other so we thought it a much better investment to put it into God's hands in the first place.

We are bombarded daily with legitimate appeals for money for some good cause like Bible distribution, keeping a Christian radio station on the air, the plight of refugees, starving children in Africa, the homeless in our neighbourhood, and even abused animals. I find it difficult to know how to respond to these. It is easy to become hardened and to feel overwhelmed. The needs presented are always much larger than what I feel I can respond to.

What helps us is to try and be sensitive to the Holy Spirit's direction and only give in obedience to God. When a specific financial appeal is made at church for example, we ask God whether we should give or not and then how much. Because He is a generous God, He will often say yes and prompt us to give more than we would have done naturally. If God says 'no' then we don't give and don't feel guilty about it. He can meet that need without us. Being sensitive when not to give is just as much a test as giving in obedience to God. There have been times when I have wanted to meet a need presumptuously out of panic or a sense of responsibility when God has stopped me from giving and I have seen a miracle unfold before my eyes.

One such incident happened with a young Norwegian man, Bjorn Seljebotten, who was serving on our ministry team in Africa. He needed to return to Norway for military service. Weeks before he was due to report for duty he asked me as his leader to pray about the timing of his flight back home. I felt to suggest to him that he travel on the same inexpensive flight via Luxembourg with a group of people that were going to attend the YWAM School in Switzerland.

The day before the flight was to leave he approached me again and asked if I still felt he should be on that flight. I unhesitatingly said 'yes' as I had no reason to think otherwise. He then told me that he did not have any money for the flight – I had presumed that coming from a wealthy nation like Norway he had no financial issues – and besides the flight was full and he had been placed on the standby list. We both agreed to continue trusting God that he could be on the flight the next day and to meet up again at the airport a few hours before the departure time.

The next day I found Bjorn outside the airlines ticket office in the airport terminal. No provision had come for his ticket overnight and he was still on the standby list. I was slightly unnerved and tried to scrounge some money together between the few of us seeing people off but to no avail. I continued to help the group leaving for Switzerland check in their luggage and then wave them goodbye at passport control. One of them, Mike Killen, already through immigration apologetically passed me an envelope that he had almost forgotten about and said that it was a gift for our ministry.

I was thrilled to find a wad of notes in the envelope and proceeded to walk to the area where I knew Bjorn was waiting, thinking that God had surely cut it fine this time. I then very clearly and almost disappointingly heard God say to me 'This money is not for him.' I needed to hear that very clearly and succinctly as I was responding out of a sense of responsibility and slight panic. Just then a young girl,

Thelma Brooderyk, approached me. She had bought travellers cheques that day as she also was going to attend a YWAM school and offered to buy Bjorn's ticket, anonymously. Without him knowing, I accompanied her to the bank to cash the traveller's cheques.

As I approached the ticket office Bjorn was standing talking to Cecilia and some friends with his back to me. I was still a few yards away when the agent beckoned him into the office to purchase his ticket. There had been a cancellation. He picked up his backpack and approached the desk still not knowing where the money was going to come from. We arrived at the desk simultaneously and I could hand the agent the money. I hardly had time to explain to Bjorn what had happened, as he needed to rush on board the plane that was ready to depart.

I am confident that Bjorn was strengthened in his faith through that incident. I, in turn, was humbled by the lesson that God can work without me. I don't need to act out of presumption or panic to bail people out financially. My responsibility is to give or not give in obedience to God.

Laziness and Irresponsibility

When it comes to a work ethic, this is my motto: *We live by faith, we don't loaf by faith.*

I believe in putting in a good day's work, not to earn God's favour but because I already have His favour and I enjoy what I am doing. We don't have to perform to be loved by God – He already loves us unconditionally as much as He ever will. But we better put our shoulder to the wheel in co-operation with God to see His rule established in the hearts of people.

God does not condone laziness and irresponsibility but does reward diligence and commitment. God has called us to work but not to make work our god. There are two extremes that I deliberately avoid. The one is boredom. I don't allow myself to get bored for more than a few minutes. There is too much living to do, so I get on with it. The other is burnout. I don't believe that we ever need to become workaholics or get burnt out, especially not in ministry. I endeavour to pace my life in such a way that I am never functioning on empty or reserve.

Tent Making

The concept of 'tent making' comes from the example of the apostle Paul who used to make tents on his expansive missionary journeys. He did not only do it to support himself and his ministry and the needs of the wider community but also to demonstrate that work in itself is a necessary and legitimate way of witnessing to Christ. All our vocations should be dedicated to living out godly Kingdom principles, no matter what sphere of society we are involved in.

Cecilia and I have been able to supplement our family's income from time to time with 'tent making' opportunities.

However, we never did these at the expense of our ministry responsibilities. They were always confined to short-term projects or a few days a month. Cecilia, for example, helped occasionally with the catering at a Christian retreat centre over a period of five years when we lived in Pretoria. From time to time I would take on small steel manufacturing jobs to provide additional funds for the family. It also created employment and a needed income for some of the missionaries we were training.

Sowing and Reaping

Growth in the Kingdom of God comes through sowing and reaping. Like good farmers we are planting seeds of faith every time we invest our time or money in an individual, a ministry or a business venture. Ultimately only God knows what will happen to every seed.

Sowing and reaping is a solid biblical principle. God gives us both seed to eat and seed to plant. It is a very foolish farmer that eats up all his seed. You cannot expect a harvest if you have no seed in the soil. Generosity is an integral part of the character of God and it should be of ours. We need to be generous not only financially, but with our time, ministry, talents, and hospitality. Being generous in these ways in obedience to God is never a poor investment.

The Sunday before my 60th birthday, Cecilia and I were invited to minister at a church in London pastored by a young Nigerian couple, Rex and Erhi Akpojaro. I had met Rex as a single man in part-time ministry. We met together regularly in what became a mentoring relationship. I prayed with him for his wife. Cecilia and I helped prepare them for marriage and I had the privilege of officiating at their wedding. We have subsequently blessed two of their children as they dedicated them to God.

Pastor Rex had wanted to bless us with a holiday for our ruby wedding anniversary and had asked the congregation to contribute to that end. He profusely thanked me for the father I had been to him and for the investment that Cecilia and I had made in their lives as a couple and in the life of the church. He quoted an Old Testament scripture saying, 'Your sons will return to you carrying gold' and assured me that he was one of those sons and hoped that there would be many more. He had wanted to insist that we holiday in Florida, apparently one of his favourite spots, but his wife convinced him otherwise, so he left the choice of venue up to us. The gift was substantial enough for us to celebrate our anniversary with a seven-day Mediterranean cruise. What a blessing!

Asking

Sometimes our needs are not met simply because we haven't bothered to ask in prayer. To presume on God's provision and blessing without asking Him is based in pride and arrogance. To acknowledge our need of Him and to ask for our needs to be met is an act of humility.

Jesus told His followers that their Heavenly Father knew their needs even before they asked Him but still instructed them to pray 'Give us today our daily bread' (Matthew 6:11). The further biblical teaching is that 'You do not have because you do not ask God' (James 4:2) or 'When you ask, you do not receive, because you ask with wrong motives, that you may spend what you get on your pleasures' (James 4:3).

There are different ways in which we can pray. Supplication is when we plead for God's mercy and grace. Petitioning is when we bring our personal requests or daily needs before God. Intercession is when we pray for the needs of others. Giving thanks is obvious.

While it is important to humbly bring our personal needs and requests to God regularly, as an acknowledgement of our dependence on Him, I have similarly learnt that the more I pray for the needs of others the less time I need to petition God for my own needs.

Pledging

When we are praying, and trusting God for financial provision for some project or vision He will often challenge us to be the answer to our own prayers. We cannot expect God to provide finances if we are not willing to give ourselves. Expecting Him to do what we are not willing to do is presumptuous and disrespectful. We do the possible and He does the impossible. He doesn't expect us to do His part, the impossible, but He does expect us to do our part.

When we bought the YWAM property in Namibia in 1980 to serve as a training centre, Cecilia and I were challenged to trust God personally and pledge five percent of the purchase price. We did so in faith and obedience not knowing where the money would come from. It certainly was not in our regular budget. God provided for us in such a way that we could meet our obligation within months of making that commitment.

When YWAM was praying for, and trusting God for, the launch of the Mercy Ships we, as a couple, were challenged to commit a month's income and a substantial amount each month for a year. The challenge seemed daunting but we committed to do so. Within a few months God had provided and we could settle our pledge in full.

Debt

We avoid debt like the plague. The Bible doesn't teach that debt is a sin, but that it is unwise. The biblical principle is simply to 'owe no one anything except to love one another' (Romans 13:8a NKJV). Cecilia and I both grew up in families that were averse to debt. We carried those principles into our marriage and decided to always live within our means and not to get into debt. Going to bed at night with the knowledge that you are not indebted to anyone makes you feel privileged and wealthy.

It is not always possible to buy expensive items without financing. In these cases, we have regarded debt as an overdue payment. Whenever we have needed financing to buy a home, for example, we have made sure that we had God's permission to do so. We have also been careful not to fall behind on any payment. In fact, we have always tried to pay more than the minimum on our mortgage and it has inevitably paid dividends in the long run. We do use credit cards for travel purposes and the occasional internet purchase but never for basic needs such as food and clothing and we clear them at the end of each month.

Getting out of debt is never easy. Filing for bankruptcy to make a new start seems like a way out but is never the credible solution. God expects us to live up to our obligations and to repay any money that we borrow. We have always encouraged people who have gotten themselves into debt to 'step up to the debt' as a matter of priority. When they have taken responsibility, and confronted their debts with an attitude of serious commitment to God, and done all that they possibly could they have seen God do what they deemed impossible and free them from debt much sooner than they had anticipated.

Stewardship

God entrusts things to us. Whether our portion is a lot or a little is for Him to decide. Our concern is to manage whatever He entrusts to us wisely and responsibly. Integrity is the standard by which Christian stewardship is measured, not only in personal and church finances but also in how we conduct business and fulfil our civic duty to pay taxes.

The basic biblical principles of good stewardship are first, being faithful in the little things. God looks at how we handle the little before He entrusts much to us. Secondly, being faithful with material things before being entrusted with spiritual riches. God looks at the way we handle objects in our care to see if we can be trusted with spiritual gifts. And thirdly, being faithful with other people's possessions to see if we can be trusted with our own (Luke 16:10-12).

I believe, for example, that God has always allowed me to have good reliable vehicles because of the way I treated my dad's cars and looked after those that I have borrowed. That includes the management of the vehicles of the mission under my care. Cecilia and I have always been meticulous to treat our accommodation in a mission community or rented accommodation as our own and leave it in a better state than we found it.

Planning financially for future contingencies is not a lack of faith but wisdom. Joseph was hailed a hero in Egypt for storing up food for the seven years of famine in the land. It led to the survival of his parents and siblings. In the book of Proverbs we are encouraged to observe the ants for being industrious and planning for the future very naturally (Proverbs 6:6). An essential part of our financial planning is to keep trusting God, be wise, and not become self-sufficient.

Gratitude

It is always a great challenge when we need a substantial financial breakthrough and we receive a seemingly small and insignificant contribution towards that need. The test is twofold.

The first test is gratitude. Will we be thankful for the little or despise the smallness of the provision? Remember, Jesus affirmed a widow for putting the equivalent of a penny or a cent – the smallest available coin– into the temple offering. She had given everything she had. Jesus recognised her not so much for what she had given but for what she had left – nothing (Mark 12:41-43).

The second test is that of faithfulness. Will we be a good steward of the little or just waste it away and not apply it for the purpose for which it was given? It is our responsibility to use money for the purpose for which it was designated.

Part of my almost daily protocol is to reflect over the past 24 hours and to thank God for His protection, provision, intervention, guidance, blessing, and favour over that period. Not only does it give me lots of fuel for praise and worship and cause for humility but it engenders faith and courage to remain dependant on God and to trust Him for the challenges lying ahead.

Enemy Activity

The enemy will often hold up finances that legally belong to you through the irresponsibility and negligence of others or through unnecessary bureaucratic red tape. We have found in times like this to affirm our position as children of God in submission to the Lordship of Christ and then to take authority over the enemy and command him to take his fingers off what is legitimately ours.

Breaking Financial Barriers for Others

We learnt early on in ministering with teams that as leaders we could break financial barriers for team members by being generous. If we believed that someone should be on our team and if we believed in their ministry and the calling upon their lives then any finances invested on our part would make a massive statement in the spirit. As we did the little, it was as if the cork came out of the bottle and God was released to do the much and allow the provision to flow.

In 1979 Cecilia and I were leading an outreach team of twenty-one people on a six-week mission to Thailand, Taiwan, Hong Kong, and Japan. In Japan we were going to participate in the YWAM outreach during the Junior World Cup football tournament. The night before we were due to leave the YWAM base was hosting a Love Feast at which we were going to be prayed for and sent out. Three of the team still needed a substantial amount for the costs involved, and were due to be bumped from the trip. After a time of communion, Ian Muir, the base director, expressed that he wanted to see the whole team go debt-free and explained that just as Jesus took our sins on Him, he wanted the community to take the outstanding debt of the team on them so that all twenty-one could leave together.

Ian then duly invited the three to the front and asked the community to pray about who they should give to and how much. They could then pay the money into the YWAM account and release the team to go debt free. I breathed a big sigh of relief knowing that the burden had shifted from me and that the finances would be provided for.

I was immediately convicted that as the leader I had a responsibility to participate in the giving. Although Cecilia and I had our outreach costs paid for we had no reserve funds. I felt to approach one of the ladies still in need and asked her what she still owed - it was about fifty percent of the full cost – and then told her to sit down explaining that from that moment on it was my responsibility and no longer hers. She immediately ran out of the hall and went to call her parents in another city to let them know she was leaving for the Far East the next morning.

As the YWAM base was going to stand in for the amount owed I thought that I would go on the outreach and on my return spend the next few months paying off the commitment. By the very next morning, before we left for the airport, I had already settled the debt with the YWAM office; I had the equivalent amount in cash as a contingency fund for the team's incidental expenses as well as the same amount as personal spending money for Cecilia and me. Wow! What a turnaround. God had provided three times the amount I had committed, and within hours.

Honour the LORD with your wealth, with the first fruits of all your crops; then your barns will be filled to overflowing, and your vats will brim over with new wine (Proverbs 3:9,10).

oOo

Chapter 13
Lambs Among Wolves

Go! I am sending you like lambs among wolves.
Luke 10:3

You don't overcome darkness
by cursing the darkness.
You overcome it by
turning on the light!

In Luke 10:3, just after Jesus had asked His disciples to pray to the Lord of the harvest to send out labourers into the harvest, He gives them an extraordinary commission: 'Go! I am sending you out like lambs among wolves'. He was not throwing them to the wolves and lions of the world to be devoured. He was not abandoning them to hardship and suffering for the sake of the gospel. He was teaching them not to respond in conflict situations in the same spirit as the spirit of the conflict but rather to respond in the way He would have responded. In a Christ-like spirit! Jesus represents the spirit of the lamb, the spirit of meekness and humility. The light of the world. The wolf represents the spirit of the world, the spirit of pride and arrogance. The spirit of darkness.

Only hours before Jesus had given His disciples this remarkable instruction, to be lambs among wolves, they had been involved in a conflict in a Samaritan village. The Samaritans had seemingly not been very hospitable to Jesus and His party and had given them the cold shoulder as they passed through their town. Nothing more than that! No stoning, no cursing or spitting, just a cold shoulder. Yet two of the disciples, James and John, are so offended by the unwelcoming culture that they react in exactly the same spirit, but even more so. They want to call fire down from heaven to annihilate the wretched Samaritans. Jesus turns to them and rebukes them by saying, 'You do not know what manner of spirit you are of. For the Son of Man did not come to destroy men's lives but to save them' (Luke 9:55,56 NKJV). They wanted to fight rejection with rejection, offence with offence, and darkness with darkness. Hence the immediate strong admonition from Jesus. The reproof was still ringing in their ears just a few hours later when He sent them to respond as lambs among the wolves.

In the natural we are exactly the same as the early followers of Jesus. When we are 'crossed' or offended our instinctive reaction is to fight the wrongdoing in the same spirit as that of the wrongdoing. When someone slams a door in our face we want to kick it down; when someone swerves in front of us we want to drive them off the road; when someone wants to prove that they are right and we are wrong we react by doing the same, trying to prove that we are right and they are wrong. We try to overcome rejection with rejection; hatred with hatred; resentment with resentment; insult with insult; and affront with affront. But this only exacerbates the problem.

In July 1978 we were in Argentina for Mundial, the FIFA Football World Cup. YWAM was hosting an international outreach in the four cities where the matches were being played. We were stationed in Cordoba. We had twenty teams of about twenty people each. For three weeks these teams had gone out every day to the stadium, plazas, parks, and squares with street drama, puppets, and music. We never drew any big crowds. A few people would stand at a distance listening to the gospel presentation. Most would just walk by seemingly uninterested. We had very little effect.

Argentina had been subject to a military coup for the two previous years and was controversially being ruled by a military junta. The nation was understandably proud of being allowed to host the World Cup and everyone was putting his or her best foot forward. The well-dressed locals would parade the streets as if on the catwalk and seemed not to want to be associated with what we were doing.

After three weeks of very little impact, Dean Sherman introduced us to the principle of 'ministering in the opposite spirit'. If the atmosphere of the city was one of pride, indifference or even self-importance then we needed to identify with those things in our own hearts and repent of them rather than point the finger in judgement. Only then could we stand in the gap with authority on behalf of the people who we were reaching out to. So at the start of our fourth and final week of the outreach we did something different. Instead of our normal presentations we humbled ourselves by kneeling in prayer in the plazas and squares in twenty locations across the city.

Initially we had to overcome our own insecurity and pride in order to get down on our knees. As we repented of our own pride and arrogance and interceded for the nation it became easier to just stay on our knees in prayer. A crowd started gathering around us. When we did get up off our knees there was a fresh willingness amongst the crowd to engage in conversations about Jesus. For the rest of the week there was not only a greater openness to our evangelistic efforts but, more importantly, we learnt an important lesson: to minister in the opposite spirit to the spirit of the world.

In 1978 the average church in Cordoba had about fifty members. There were a few churches in town with 200 members. My responsibility was to place the twenty teams in twenty different churches on the four Sundays of the outreach, so Cecilia and I spent a lot of time visiting pastors. Church growth in Argentina was very small for many decades and then in the 1980s and 1990s Argentina saw phenomenal church growth. The graph of church growth shows an almost flat line for many years and then a turning point between 1978 and 1982 with exponential growth for the next two decades. Church leaders attribute this to Argentina losing the war over the Falklands in 1982. They believe that the nations spirit of national pride and arrogance was broken. The country was humbled and it ushered in revival.

Discernment

We are spiritual beings having a short human experience. We are much more discerning than we give ourselves credit for. You don't have to be a rocket scientist to feel the change in atmosphere as you travel from one nation to another or relocate from the suburbs to the inner part of the same city. At times, you may be going about your daily tasks in a normal way and suddenly experience a spirit of fear, or uncharacteristic sexual thoughts, or uncanny feelings of insignificance and timidity. What probably is happening is that your spiritual radar is picking up the pervasive spirit of the atmosphere of the place you are in. Instead of submitting to that spirit and becoming anxious, or lustful, or intimidated you respond in the opposite spirit and declare your trust in God, celebrate your purity and identity in Christ.

I was once explaining the opposite spirit principle as a guest in a home group led by friends of ours. He interrupted me and explained that he had an illustration of the principle from an experience just a few weeks earlier. He was an academic and his pet activity was to research cults and false religions and prepare himself to refute their arguments and to be a 'defender of the faith'. He told of a young couple that arrived at his door wanting to offer him a particular magazine and try to engage in conversation. He immediately recognised them as from a group that deny that Jesus is Jehovah albeit recognising Him as a prophet and a good man. He enthusiastically invited them in, asked his wife to make them some tea, and hastened to his study to find his notes on their specific arguments. For the next thirty to forty minutes they were engaged in a heated discussion, arguing back and forth, and not making any headway.

At that point, my friend's wife interjected and apologised for interrupting the lively debate and explained that what she was about to say had nothing to do with the argument at hand. She asked the young wife about a detailed hurtful incident that had happened recently and assured her that God loved her and knew all about it. Both the guests' jaws dropped open in surprise. There was no way our friend could have known such intimate detail about the lady. They knew it had to be supernatural and were deeply touched by the compassion and sensitivity with which they were ministered to. Our friends could introduce them to Jesus and help them engage in a dynamic relationship with Him. They left that evening being real witnesses for Jehovah, witnessing to the transforming power of Jesus Christ in their lives.

My friend concluded by saying that he was so embarrassed by the course of action he had taken, thinking that he could win an argument with them. He had submitted to their spirit of religious controversy and was approaching them in the same spirit of religious argument.

His wife had responded in the spirit of Christ and was able to turn on the light and minister life. Rather lose an argument and accomplish something for eternity than win an argument as another notch on your belt.

We were once camped in Istanbul for ten days preparing for a visit to some Eastern European nations. The oppressive nature and fatalistic spirit of the city was palpable. When we crossed the border from Turkey into Bulgaria we were surprised by remarkable change in the atmosphere. It was like coming into a free open space. It didn't take us long, however, to discern that the spirit of socialism was much subtler and deceiving.

I have been in places where I have been aware of a spirit of lust and immorality. You could almost smell it in the atmosphere. I then immediately resist the temptation, focus on the loving, satisfying intimate relationship I have with Cecilia, and choose to respond in a spirit of purity. Cecilia and I have walked the red-light district of Amsterdam together after being taught by Floyd McClung to represent the life and light of Christ and not to be fascinated by the allure of the area. I have been a guest of their ministry house called The Cleft with a Satanist temple and a brothel as their respective neighbours without succumbing to the intimidation and temptations that they represented.

We cannot resolve conflicts by responding in the same spirit as that of the conflict. We have to respond in the spirit of Christ, which is often directly opposite to our natural inclination. Rejection is not resolved by more rejection or self-pity. Hatred is not resolved by responding in bitterness and resentment. Disappointments are not erased by blaming God and others. The effect of criticism is not nullified by reacting and criticizing the critic. We need to be open to the conviction of the Holy Spirit and respond in humility with a magnanimous spirit as Christ would have.

Being Jesus to the World

Being lambs among wolves simply means rightly representing Jesus in the world. His life is the light of the world not ours. When we represent His love and His attitudes of humility, mercy, and servanthood we are being the light of the world.

oOo

Chapter 14
Going Barefoot

Whoever wants to become great among you must be
your servant, and whoever wants to be first must be
slave of all. For even the Son of Man did not
come to be served, but to serve, and to
give his life as a ransom for many.
Mark 10:43-45

Freedom is not the ability to 'do your own thing'.
That is licence which leads to bondage.
True freedom is the ability to do
what you know is right.

In biblical times a servant or slave would always go barefoot in the presence of his master. This was a sign of subservience, honour and respect. To appear in the presence of your master with sandals or shoes on your feet would be a sign of disrespect and a lack of subordination.

When Paul writes to the church in Philippi he explains to them that Jesus, although being in very nature God did not hold onto that equality with God but was willing to relinquish all the glory of heaven to come to earth and take on the nature of a man in the form of a slave. The Greek word used here is doulos, which simply means slave, nothing more and nothing less. 'Christ was truly God. But he did not try to remain equal with God. Instead he gave up everything and became a slave, when he became like one of us' (Philippians 2:6,7 CEV).

In ancient times you became a slave primarily as a result of the spoils of war - those that weren't killed were sold as slaves - or as the sentence for a crime. A slave-master would choose a slave (at the slave market), would buy the slave, would own the slave, would take care of the slave's needs, would discipline the slave, and would reward the slave. When the time came for a slave to be set free, either by completing his sentence or at the discretion of a benevolent master, he would be given the option to take his freedom or to stay on loyally serving his master. If he chose the latter his master would pierce his ear with an awl and give him a ring to wear for all to see that he was bonded to the master by choice, hence the term bondservant or bondslave. The slave still remained subject to the master.

As Free as a Slave

I like to talk about being 'as free as a slave' – it sounds contradictory but it's not. When you hear the word 'slavery' you don't think of freedom but of bondage, hardship, suffering, restrictions, and imprisonment. For me it conjures up images from the movie Ben-Hur of galley slaves being chained hand and foot to the thick oars of a warship and rowing it into battle.

True freedom only comes when we are truly the servant or bondslave of Jesus Christ, totally surrendered to His Lordship. The implication is that we are then no longer the slave of anything or anybody else. We are then no longer the slave of past sin, guilt or shame. We are not the slave of time, money, fear or the devil. We are not the slave of anything or anybody else, and that is true freedom.

The principle is actually quite simple. We maintain our responsibility to do what we know to be right by having an attitude of submission to our Master. We then defer the rest to Him. A slave never had to worry unduly about where he would live or what he would eat or wear. That was the master's responsibility. If he had an abusive master he was in trouble. If he had a kind and generous master he had it made. We know who the best master is!

Our Master Jesus calls us His friends. 'You are my friends if you do what I command' (John 15:14). He does not only call us friends but sons and daughters and makes us joint heirs with Him too. He chose us, bought us with a great price, owns us, teaches and disciplines us, and abundantly takes care of all our needs. That is a Master that I can lay down my life for.

Going Barefoot

In the third chapter of Exodus Moses is confronted by a burning bush that is not consumed by the fire. As he approaches it with curiosity he hears the stern voice of an angel commanding him to take the shoes off his feet because the ground he is standing on is holy (Exodus 3:5). He realises that he is in God's presence. He takes off his shoes in respect and bows his head to the ground in worship. Moses would have been familiar with servants and slaves going barefoot in Pharaoh's palace. He subsequently receives instructions from God for the deliverance of His people from Egypt.

Joshua had a comparable experience when confronted by 'the captain of the Lord's army' with a similar instruction to take the shoes off his feet because he was on holy ground. The angel then proceeds to give him instructions for the conquering of Jericho (Joshua 5:13-15).

King David had to flee from Jerusalem after his son Absalom had conspired against him and led a rebellion to remove him from the throne. David left the city weeping with his head covered in shame and he went barefoot (2 Samuel 15:30). Absalom was subsequently killed in the ensuing battle and David was re-instated to the throne. We can similarly go through difficult times of betrayal without being crushed if we are totally surrendered to God. If we go barefoot.

Early on in Joshua's leadership God promised him that every place that the sole of his feet trod upon – where he was surrendered and subservient - he would receive as an inheritance (Joshua 1:3 NKJV). The New Testament equivalent of this principle is found in the Sermon on the Mount or Beatitudes. Here Jesus makes the promise 'Blessed are the meek, for they will inherit the earth' (Matthew 5:5).

Meekness, yielding our will to God's will while having an attitude of subservience and respect for Him - going barefoot - is the key to inheriting all that God has for us.

Total Surrender

The most basic principle of Christian discipleship is found in the Gospel of Mark. Here Jesus challenges us to a wholehearted and total surrender to His Lordship. 'Whoever wants to be my disciple must deny themselves and take up their cross and follow me. For whoever wants to save their life will lose it, but whoever loses their life for me and for the gospel will save it' (Mark 8:34,35).

God blesses us with many gifts and privileges. The gift of family, friends, and freedom. With natural abilities and talents. With spiritual gifts and ministry opportunities. The gifts of work and things. The privilege of adventure and travel. The gift of life itself. We can regard these as our entitlement, if we like, or regard them as privileges and yield them to God. If we grasp hold of any of these 'rights' in a selfish way, we lose them. The only way to truly secure them is to surrender or relinquish them to God.

In his book Winning God's Way (later published under the title Making Jesus Lord) Loren Cunningham explains the concept of 'relinquishment of rights'. A slave had no rights of his own, they belonged to the master. There were also certain things that the slave was not responsible for, they were the master's responsibility. The only responsibility the slave had was to serve his master. If we maintain our responsibility towards God but give up our right to these privileges then we will inherit the reward of relationship with Him and more fully enjoy His blessings.

We always maintain our responsibility towards our family and friends and need to be reliable stewards of our abilities, talents, and resources. But we don't treat them as our possessions. We don't hold on to them with a clenched fist but with an open hand. We entrust them to God.

Jesus lived this principle. He completely fulfilled His responsibility in coming to earth. On the cross, He could declare 'It is finished!' (John 19:30). He had done what He came to do. In doing so He gave up every conceivable right.

He gave up being God to become a man. He gave up all the wonder and splendour of heaven to live on a dusty earth. He gave up His reputation at birth, being deemed illegitimate. He was born in a lowly place amongst the animals and into a despised race, under Roman occupation. He willingly took on the form of a servant to mankind laying aside all the rights that people took for granted. Even while suffering an agonizing death on the cross and being mocked He gave up the right to call on the power of God to destroy the world and set Him free. Jesus didn't even have His own grave. They had to borrow a tomb for Him to be buried in. He 'walked barefoot' from the cradle to the grave. He literally walked barefoot to the cross.

What does God do? He rewards Jesus with all power and authority. He exalts Jesus to the highest place of honour. He gives Him a name that is above every name so that at the name of Jesus every knee shall bow and every tongue shall confess that Jesus Christ is Lord (Philippians 2:9,10).

If we want to inherit all that God has for us we need to live the way Jesus did, yielded to God, walking barefoot.

Personal Application

Whenever I am impatient, irritated, frustrated, discontent or angry for more than a few minutes or unduly worried about something then I know I am in trouble. None of these attitudes are the 'attitude of Christ' that we are meant to emulate. They always indicate a lack of freedom in some area. They cause me to stop in my tracks. When I pause to reflect I am inevitably confronted with something I have to let go off, some right that I have retained that needs relinquishing.

It has sometimes been as simple as being impatient in congested traffic and giving up 'my right' to be at my destination speedily. I can then enjoy the tranquillity that follows and use the time to reflect, pray or meditate. At other times it has been frustration and irritation that my plans for the day have been scuppered by some unexpected need or 'emergency'. Giving up my right to 'my time' frees me for God to use me to serve others as He wants.

Here are some more examples of how this principle of relinquishment has played out in our lives.

Travelling

There were seasons that I travelled a lot and was away from home often. I had to balance my leadership and ministry responsibilities with my family responsibilities. But I had to give up the right to always be with my family or always have them with me. And they likewise had to release me for the sake of the Kingdom of God.

Our family 'travel policy' at that time was that I would limit being away from home to thirty percent of the year. I would try to never be away for more than a week at a time and preferably be home for the weekends. I would only have two trips per year of up to three weeks long that only include two weekends away. And we as a family would travel together as much as practically possible

There was only one occasion that I was separated from Cecilia and Cindy-Joy for a period of five weeks while on an extensive 'Keith Green Memorial Tour' with Floyd McClung and Melody Green through seven states in the USA. It was a recruitment drive for missions in honour of Keith Green, who had been killed in a plane crash with eleven other people including two of his children. Keith and Melody Green were the leaders of Last Days Ministries and both song writers. Keith was a contemporary Christian artist and at the time of his death was well-known for his strong devotion to evangelism and missions. His songs particularly challenged others to do the same. Melody had felt it right to go ahead with two concert tours that had already been planned prior to the accident. I had the privilege of being on one of these tours of nineteen concerts. A video recording of Keith's last concert was played, Melody would share her testimony, one of us 'missionaries' would be interviewed, and Floyd would give an impassioned challenge for missions. We saw hundreds respond to the mission call and dozens commit their lives to Christ each night.

Cecilia was very good at teaching the children that they were privileged to have a daddy that worked for God and was away on His business. They invested in my ministry trips by often praying for me at the evening meal or at bedtime while I was away. My arrivals back home were always very special as I was greeted with lots of loving hugs and enthusiastic 'Daddy what did you bring us?' Followed by my reply of 'I brought you (pause) ME!' And then the inevitable 'Ah!'

The rewards are too numerous to mention. God has given us back to one another in deep loving relationships that are unimaginable. When I was not travelling I had the privilege to work from home, which made me more available and accessible to the family than would otherwise have been the case. In 1994, we as a family of six had an amazing four-month sabbatical in the USA as part of a recognition for twenty-one years in missions. We travelled through twenty-two states, made many friends, and built lasting memories. Another blessing was that we often had the privilege of travelling together.

In 1974 during our Middle East field trip Cecilia and I were camped in Istanbul, Turkey preparing for a visit behind the so-called Iron Curtain. We had a visa for Bulgaria, the next country on our route, but needed a visa for Romania to continue our journey back towards Germany. While our visa application for Romania was being processed for a week God challenged us to forfeit the right to go behind the Iron Curtain by relinquishing the right to use our Bulgarian visa, which He had already miraculously provided. That was hard! We had to check our motives for wanting to go behind the Iron Curtain. Was it out of a sense of adventure and intrigue about communism or was it to do what God wanted and to please Him? We relinquished the Bulgarian visa back to God.

Only then were we free in our hearts to either turn back from Istanbul, if need be, without any resentment in our hearts or to proceed with the plan if God made the way. The outcome was that the Romanian visa was granted and our sojourn behind the Iron Curtain could go ahead with the resulting profound and pivotal impact on our lives.

In 1979 Cecilia and I were travelling in South America ministering for a week each at the YWAM base in Buenos Aires, Argentina; Belo Horizonte, Brazil; Santiago, Chile; and Bogota, Columbia. After that we were scheduled to be in Los Angeles, USA, for ten days before returning to South Africa via Frankfurt, Germany.

Before leaving South Africa we had secured visas for Argentina, Brazil, Chile, and the USA but were unsuccessful in obtaining one for Columbia. We tried for Columbian visas again in Argentina and Brazil and were turned down. Having a visa for Columbia was crucial to our flights working out. As a last gasp attempt I went to the Columbian

Embassy in Santiago, Chile only to be told in no uncertain terms by the Columbian diplomat that they don't even consider visa applications from South African citizens. In fact, they had an order from Bogota not to forward any such applications to headquarters.

Our visa application for Columbia had been rejected for the fourth time. It was time to 'relinquish our rights' again. We had to put our desire to minister in Columbia and to visit the USA for the first time on the altar.

That evening as I was ministering to the YWAM community of about thirty young people I told them the situation and asked for prayer. One of the young lads started praying from Proverbs 21:1: 'The king's heart is in the hand of the Lord like the rivers of water; He turns it wherever He wishes'. He prayed for God's favour at the Columbian Embassy.

The next morning the school secretary went to the Columbian Embassy on our behalf and returned by lunchtime with visas in our passports issued 'courtesy of the ambassador in Chile'. He had taken it upon himself to issue the visas. God had turned his heart. A great outcome again but only after we had maintained our responsibility by doing the possible and yielding our 'rights' to God again.

In the 1980s I was invited by a group of leaders in South Africa to attend a Christian conference in Singapore. All expenses and flights were paid for and I was to be given a daily allowance for incidental needs and expenses. I had never had it that easy financially. All I had to do was pack my bags and apply for the visa, which I dutifully did. A week before the departure date there was no visa. The day before departure, no visa. An hour before the flight was due to leave, still no visa and the flight left without me. My seat remained unused. Although I was deeply disappointed as I waved my friends goodbye at the airport, my life wasn't shattered. I had relinquished the prospect of attending the conference from the outset and was able to get on with living life to the full despite not going.

Family

Cecilia and I often had to relinquish the desire or right to have children back to God or in religious parlance to 'put it on the altar' as an offering to God. Cecilia particularly had to face the disappointment month after month. She handled it impeccably well with an air of quiet confidence and a firm trust in God.

In scanning through my journals, I noticed an entry on 3 April 1980 in which I expressed my disappointment and frustration at the lack of progress in our application to be adoptive parents. The welfare services had called me to say that they were still awaiting an independent report from a social worker on our financial situation (complicated because we had no guaranteed income or pay slips to submit). The 'note to self' stated that the frustration and disappointment I experienced was an indication that I was not relinquished in that particular facet of my life but subtly demanding. I had already learnt the lesson that any reaction of impatience, frustration, anger or similar was an indication of an area of bondage, of not walking barefoot in that specific aspect, and thus not enjoying freedom as a result.

The next day, 4 April 1980, was Good Friday. As I reflected on the sacrificial death of Jesus on the cross for us I wrote in my journal 'This day I relinquish the right to ever have a child. I give it back to the Lord.

I will not continue demanding the privilege of sharing my life with a child or children. I will however, be grateful, very grateful, should God see fit to give us a child – whenever!'

Three months later, at a group session with two other couples, we were informed that we had been approved as adoptive parents and told that all we needed to do now was wait. The social worker did add a disclaimer by saying that some couples would wait a long time and some may wait until 'Jesus returns'. We understood that to mean a long time, and again relinquished our growing desire to be parents back to God in order to avoid any disappointment.

We were also in the midst of packing for a permanent move to Windhoek South West Africa/Namibia. My journal entry that day reads, 'Lord Jesus we trust you to work it out so that our move to SWA does not cause any further complications or delays in the adoption process. Lord I trust you for a miracle in providing us with the right child at the right time'.

Within less than five months, on 25 November 1980, we became the very proud adopters of the most beautiful three-week-old baby girl with deep blue eyes and jet-black hair.

As our family grew from three to five and eventually to six we had to keep relinquishing our four children back to God knowing full well that He could take good care of them and had only entrusted them to us for a season.

When our youngest son David was six weeks old he contracted a bone marrow infection – osteomyelitis - in his right leg. Cecilia was breastfeeding him at the time and insisted on spending the forty days in hospital with him while he received antibiotics intravenously. Initially it was touch and go whether they would amputate his little leg. The leg was saved and the infection cleared after two sets of surgery. Today he bears a scar down the full length of his lower leg as a reminder that he could have been without that limb had it not been for the grace of God and excellent medical intervention.

After watching a film on the life of Hudson Taylor I remember being challenged by the fact that he lost his wife and two children on the mission field. I would find it very hard to see Cecilia or any of our children or grandchildren die. That would be difficult. In prayer, I often find myself having to relinquish them all back to God and commit myself not to become resentful or bitter should that ever happen. Only then can I fully enjoy my relationship with them and be free of the fear of what the future may hold.

Even now, at the time of writing, I am acutely aware of the need to hold onto our children and four grandchildren lightly - with an open hand rather than a clenched fist - and entrust them into the hand of God for His care and keeping.

Ministry Opportunities

In 1984 Cecilia and I were pioneering YWAM in the Western Cape, South Africa. We had our second adoption pending. I had been appointed Assistant Regional Director for Southern Africa as I was still overseeing the work in Namibia. I had felt called to serve and support Ian Muir, the Regional Director in developing the work in Southern Africa. On the same day that I was invited to be a member of the Europe, Middle East and Africa Council (EMAC) for YWAM I was also invited to consider a leadership role for YWAM in New Zealand. Both the invitations came from men I respected and had a high regard for. What do you do? You relinquish everything. You lay it all down and ask God what responsibilities He wants you to pick up. Where does He want you to serve?

It only took a few days for Cecilia and me to get complete clarity and consensus. We had no peace about New Zealand. We had learnt never to ignore a lack of peace. God confirmed our calling to pioneer the Western Cape and to continue to serve the vision of YWAM in Southern Africa. As part of my leadership role in Africa I was then able to serve on the EMAC for YWAM, which met a few times a year somewhere in Europe, the Middle East or Africa under the leadership of Floyd McClung.

Unbeknown to us, our twins had already been born and were entrusted to us only a few weeks later. We understood then why we had not been released to consider going to New Zealand.

From time to time I had to relinquish a leadership role or ministry title in favour of younger leaders. It sometimes didn't make sense but it was always to move on to other things in God. It has never been difficult for me as my identity has certainly not been in a position or title, but in my relationship with God. I have always held to positions lightly while taking my responsibilities very seriously. I make a distinction between carrying a baton of leadership responsibility and the call of God on my life. It is relatively easy for me to pass on my baton of responsibility or leadership to others when the time is right, but I am going to carry the flame of my calling until my dying day. I will light as many other torches as I can on the way and keep running with my flame to the end.

Mercy Ships

The ministry of Mercy Ships is an integral part of the formative years of YWAM. I have had the privilege of my journey crossing paths with that journey on numerous occasions and it has always been deeply challenging and profoundly transformative. My life has been greatly enriched by it and for that I am extremely grateful.

When Cecilia and I joined the YWAM School of Evangelism in Lausanne, Switzerland in 1974 we learnt of the 'death of a vision' that YWAM had gone through in the previous few months. In September 1973 YWAM had paid the deposit on the Maori, a New Zealand inter-island ferry, with a commitment to pay the balance in thirty days. She was large enough to serve the vision that had been brewing for years of a medical ship. She would be manned by hundreds of volunteers, serving the medical needs in needy nations and disaster areas.

Over one hundred volunteers and crew were already on board the Maori getting her ready to set sail as soon as the final payment was made. In the meantime, God was speaking to the YWAM leadership that they had taken their focus off the giver in favour of the gift. Jesus had been left in the shadows with all the hype and excitement about a hunk of metal. There was a deep time of repentance and relinquishment. The balance on the Maori was never paid, the deposit was lost along with the reputation of the mission, especially in New Zealand. And the vision died.

In 1978 the dream started becoming a reality again when YWAM purchased the Victoria, an eleven-thousand-ton Italian luxury liner that had been dead in the water and ready to be sold as scrap. Once the purchase had been secured, the emblem on the funnel had been replaced with the YWAM logo and the name changed to Anastasis – resurrection.

In June 1979 I was on board the Anastasis, still anchored in the bay outside the harbour in Venice, Italy. A group of sixty International YWAM leaders had been summoned together for a few days of prayer and seeking God for the resurrection of the vision that had previously died. A generator provided electricity for the section that we used and we had to fill our own buckets overboard if we wanted to use the toilet. Very rudimentary.

The challenge of seeing the ship restored to her former glory, let alone being transformed into a floating hospital, was obviously enormous. That, plus the history of humbling and relinquishment that had gone on before, put us in a place of surrender and total dependence on God. The dream was rekindled. Fresh faith was conceived in my own heart to trust God for the impossible in my life as well.

The Anastasis was then towed to Greece where she underwent four years of painstaking upgrades and refurbishment complete with three operating theatres, a forty-bed hospital, and accommodation for 350 crew and volunteers. She set sail under the Maltese flag as the Anastasis on 7 July 1982 to minister into the acute medical needs of poor nations and to bring the resurrection life of Christ to people around the world.

In 2007 the Anastasis was replaced by the African Mercy, a converted Danish Rail Ferry. She has a ninety-bed hospital, three modern operating theatres, and a crew capacity of 450.

I have had the honour of being a guest speaker in the discipleship school on board one of the Mercy Ships many times. I have visited while the ship was in 'outreach' mode in places such as Madagascar; Dakar, Senegal; Freetown, Sierra Leone; Monrovia, Liberia; Porto Nova, Benin; and Lomé in Togo. Also, while in 'procurement' mode in Holland and the USA. I had the privilege of officially welcoming the Anastasis to Cape Town on her first of many visits to South Africa.

I found all of these inflection points with Mercy Ships to be developmental in my own journey of relinquishment. I saw, first-hand, the dedication of highly skilled medical professionals who had relinquished lucrative earnings to serve the vulnerable. I experienced some of their anguish during 'screening week' when people had to be turned away that they couldn't help. The dozens that had malaria for example or a particular condition for which the surgery slots were already filled. The need was always greater.

I also heard testimonies of deep gratitude and transformed lives at the end of a three or four-month outreach when the ship was getting ready to sail to another port. As I remembered how the vision had to die initially, I was always deeply challenged. As I saw the fruit of the ministry I was both encouraged and motivated to keep walking barefoot.

Apart from the untold thousands of people who have been helped and affected by the medical missions and relief and development outreaches of the Mercy Ships, there must be hundreds of thousands - if not millions - of people who have been involved, who have served and invested in some way. That challenges me over and over again to do my bit and to keep serving.

Vanya

Bob Ayala, a contemporary musician, was one of the performing artists on the Keith Green Memorial tour in 1983, that I was privileged to be part of. Night after night he would tell the story of a young Soviet soldier who was martyred for his faith in Christ. Vanya, or Ivan Moiseyev, had experienced many miracles such as being kept warm supernaturally while having to stand outside in the snow for many nights in sub-zero temperatures, in his summer uniform. Once he was run over by a truck. He was told his life could only be saved by the amputation of an arm and part of a collapsed lung. Delirious with fever he earnestly prayed aloud. The next morning he was completely healed. Many of Vanja's compatriots became followers of Jesus as a result of these miracles.

In 1972 Vanya's parents received a message from the military to say that their son had accidently drowned in the Black Sea and that they needed to retrieve the body for burial. Before the funeral, in his home town, his father broke open the zinc coffin to examine the body. They found evidence of extensive physical harm all over his body, including multiple stab wounds in his chest.

Bob Ayala composed a song called Vanya with striking lyrics. One verse particularly struck me every time he sang it on the memorial tour.

Vanya, they cut short your stay
But they could not take your life away
For you'd already laid it down
Before the One who had promised you a crown.
God bless you Vanya

oOo

Chapter 15
Rich Heritage

My son, do not forget my law,
But let your heart keep my commands;
For length of days and long life
And peace they will add to you.
Let not mercy and truth forsake you;
Bind them around your neck,
Write them on the tablet of your heart,
And so find favour and high esteem
In the sight of God and man.
Proverbs 3:1-4 (NKJV)

The only thing you take with you when
you're gone is what you leave behind.
John Allston

Spirit is Thicker than Blood

The concept of 'spirit is thicker than blood' has had far more implications for us than just the blessing of being a loving, accepting, close-knit family of six. It affects the way we do relationships on a far wider scale. I have experienced many deeply spiritual moments that have far exceeded the politics of the day or the bonds of culture, tribe or race and given me a small glimpse into what it might be like in the Kingdom of God.

It was 4 pm on Thursday 31 July 1997 in Kinshasa, Congo. As Dr Nico Landman and I alighted from the chauffeured Mercedes-Benz into the crowded city street and then into the church compound a tumultuous welcome erupted. Our entryway was lined with singing, dancing ladies in new colourful outfits. The dusty pathway was decked with brand-new cloth. It was humbling to walk on this expensive garment material with abject poverty all around us. We were escorted past a cheering welcome party towards the modest church building. The place was jam-packed and there was an overflow crowd outside. The beat of drums, the shrill of whistles, and the cacophony of singing, shouting, laughing people must have been heard for miles around.

The occasion was the welcoming of Dr Nico Landman from the Federal Council of the Pentecostal Protestant Church in South Africa. For fourteen years, there had been no contact between the mother church in South Africa and the planted church in the former Zaire. In the meantime, the church had flourished throughout this francophone, central-African nation. Through a set of divinely orchestrated circumstances the daughter church and the mother church had discovered each other again.

This was the historic moment of embrace again; of healing and reconciliation; of putting the past behind and facing the future hand in hand as partners. Brother Landman gave an impassioned greeting and then powerfully ministered the Word of God. An anointed atmosphere of reverence and worship settled over the audience. I moved between the pastors and elders and prayed for the anointing of God upon them to be manifest to His glory. I knelt in humility before God under the weight and the awe of the moment.

As I knelt and wept before the Lord a healing balm flooded my soul. There was a time that white South Africans were not welcomed in these nations and were hated all over Africa. The welcome we received was overwhelming. The love and acceptance was refreshing. Despite the language and cultural barriers, we had come home. Spirit is truly thicker than blood!

The prayer of Jesus in John 17, 'Father that they may be made perfect in one as we are one', was being answered before our eyes.

Another such moment was in November 1990 during the National Conference of Church Leaders at Hunters Rest in Rustenburg, South Africa. The meeting had been called 'Towards a united Christian witness in a changing South Africa'. The co-chairmen were Dr Louw Alberts, a recognised scientist, and Reverend Dr Frank Chikane, a denominational leader. I was invited as the National Director of YWAM South Africa and was attending with my close friend Francois Vosloo, the National Director of Operation Mobilisation.

In February of that year President F.W. de Klerk had made the unprecedented announcement of the unbanning of the African National Congress (ANC) and other opposition groups as well the imminent release of Nelson Mandela after twenty-seven years as a political prisoner. It ushered in a whole new chapter of uncertain anticipation in South African politics.

In October 1990 the Dutch Reformed Church (DRC) had boldly passed a resolution distancing itself from its past support of the policy of apartheid. The resolution affirmed that the 'honest and noble intention of the policy was the optimal development of all population groups within the framework of their own cultural traditions' but confessed that the implementation of the policy had become ethnocentric. 'It had become in practice racist and oppressive.' The statement concluded with a plea for the reconciliation of the entire nation (Dutch Reformed Church 'Resolution on Apartheid' 1990).

At the conference in November 1990 I was seated a few rows behind Archbishop Desmond Tutu who sat in the front row. Dr Willie Jonker, a theologian, was delivering an address on behalf of the DRC. Willie Jonker departed from his prepared paper and made a contrite personal confession of sin and responsibility for apartheid and proposed that he was speaking on behalf of the DRC and the Afrikaner people. His tone was notably repentant. I was deeply touched by his openness and vulnerability.

I was then taken slightly by surprise when Archbishop Tutu responded immediately, jumped onto the stage and with his arm around Willie Jonker's shoulder said: 'I am constrained by the Holy Spirit to forgive my brother' and then continued to confess the racism in his and in every other church. He then led the conference in a time of repentance, forgiveness, and reconciliation. It was another deeply significant and poignant spiritual moment that transcended that of tribe, race, political affiliation or church denomination. A small glimpse of what might be.

The next day, Johan Heyns, the moderator of the DRC confirmed that his denomination fully identified with Willie Jonker's confession the previous day. In spite of that, and the moving time of reconciliation under the anointing of the Holy Spirit, there were still a minority who ridiculed both the confession of Willie Jonker and Desmond Tutu's magnanimous response arguing that neither of them could speak for others but only speak in their own capacity. That might be understandable in the light of the very emotive and rapidly changing political environment at the time. I am of the conviction though, that the moment of public repentance, forgiveness, and reconciliation, however brief, went a long way to lay the foundation - and pave the way - for what transpired into peaceful general elections in April 1994.

South Africa was on the brink of civil war. The Zulus, the biggest tribe and traditional warriors, were not going to participate in the elections. The fear was that they would take up arms, albeit sticks and stones, no matter what the outcome of the elections. Through the mediation of men of God, the Zulus under the leadership of chief Buthelezi concurred to participate in the elections at the last minute.

That period is commonly referred to as the 'miracle of South Africa'. It was not just a political victory it was also a spiritual one. There were spiritual forces at work to derail the process but people were praying around the world. The miracle happened, power was transferred peacefully, civil war was averted, and a Rainbow Nation was born. South Africa is again in desperate need of such a miracle.

The Rewards of Ministry

Ministry is incredibly rewarding, despite all the challenges and occasional hardships. Cecilia and I have had the privilege of investing in thousands of people's lives, especially young people, that have gone on to effectively serve God in various capacities all over the world. I once was the guest speaker at a pastors' conference for the Pentecostal Holiness church in Zambia. My interpreter, Pastor Patrick Kawangu, introduced himself to me as one of my sons. He had attended a discipleship and missions training programme that we led in 1995. He had continued with theological training, been ordained, and was now overseeing thirty churches in the Copper Belt of Zambia. So, so rewarding and encouraging! And that story has been multiplied many times over.

A special spin-off and reward of our family story is the blessing and encouragement it has been to many other childless couples. We have prayed for, and trusted God with, many such a couple that have gone on to have families of their own. Some of them have three or four children as a monumental testimony to the goodness of God.

One of the countries I have visited the most, apart from those that we have lived in for several years, is Ukraine. I have frequented the country at least twenty times since 2005.

My first two visits were to invest in the lives of pastors from all over Eastern Europe. Lofty and Petra Nel, from Doxa Deo in South Africa had ministry links to an orphanage in Berdichev, Ukraine and would organise these conferences. Typically, we would have fifty to sixty pastors attend for five days and we would have as many as eighteen sessions of equipping and teaching during that time.

Some of the young people in our newly-started church in London wanted to go on outreach during the summer months. They were accustomed to doing such ministry trips as students. We decided that, rather than spread ourselves too thinly, to focus our efforts on Ukraine where we already had developing relationships. In 2007 we sent a team of half a dozen young people to prayer walk the City of Kiev. They were hosted by Lyudmyla (Lyuda) Ivanchenko who had served as interpreter during my previous two visits. Apart from prayer walking the city, Lyuda introduced them to a small group of people who for various reasons had been disenfranchised from mainstream church and were hurting. The group was led by Oleg and Tanya Usatyuk.

On the team's return to London, Oleg sent me an email to thank me for the team's visit to Kiev with the message: 'The young people were so natural and real and the presence of Jesus was thick amongst them'. And then appealed to us as a church to help them through the difficult season that they found themselves in.

Within a few weeks, two of us went for a short, mid-week visit to see how we could serve them. We were met by warm and friendly, quality people who were very open about their painful journey and hungry to learn. I was immediately impressed by their humble attitudes and the lack of resentment and need for vindication.

For the next three days fifteen of us sat in a small flat around a coffee table, typically laden with food, sharing life together. From 9 am to 5 pm I would field questions, teach principles, establish values, hear stories, and minister the grace of God. There was also lots and lots of prayer. I joked afterwards that the only time I got to eat something was when Lyuda was interpreting for me.

In the evenings more people would join us for worship and prayer in what they regarded as a more formal 'church service.' On the third night we had communion together – a big deal for them as this was just in an informal house setting. I only realised later that they had started seeing me then in a fatherly or 'apostolic' role. I subsequently visited the group regularly. After my third visit in quick succession I wrote the following statement in my 2008 journal, 'Oleg told me that he has learnt more in the last six months – my three short visits – than all his years in the Church. I am both encouraged and deeply saddened'. I was encouraged that he was growing spiritually and as a leader but deeply saddened at the lack of discipleship in the Church in general.

In 2008 the group recognised Oleg Usatyuk as the lead Elder that God had appointed over them and decided to call their church Bozha Slava (The Glory of God) church. I continued to visit the church between one and three times annually for the next ten years and sent others in the intervening times when I could not make it. Our role has been one of support and encouragement and spiritual development rather than anything strategic or contextual.

Oleg and Tanya Usatyuk have completed formal Bible School training and are recognised as pastors in the Ukraine Mission Union, a union of 157 churches that Bozha Slava formally belongs to. Oleg is also recognised as the head chaplain of a group of fourteen chaplains from their Union.

From 18-23 February 2014 Ukraine experienced a revolution on Independence Square (Maidan) in the heart of Kiev. It was also known as the Euromaidan Revolution or Revolution of Dignity. Many unarmed protestors were killed by unknown gunmen. It culminated in the ousting of the Ukraine President, Viktor Yanukovych, and the restoring of the Constitution of Ukraine to its 2004 form that had been repealed when Yanukovych had come to power.

On the evening of Friday 4 April Diederick Meij and I were on Maidan with our friend Oleg. It was still occupied by protestors in makeshift shelters with candle-lit 'memorials' all over the place signifying the spots where dozens of people had been indiscriminately shot. The churches were manning a 24/7 prayer vigil for the nation. There were about twenty of us standing in a circle praying when I was handed a microphone and told to publicly bring greetings from London. I did so and asserted that the city and nation needed the grace of God more than ever and declared that 'God gives grace to the humble!' I emphasised that we could activate or trigger the grace of God by acknowledging Him and humbling ourselves before Him. One of the ways we demonstrate our humility is by kneeling before him. I then instinctively knelt in the dirt – all the paving had been lifted to use as weapons and barricades during the protests – and to my surprise all those standing in the prayer circle, including a uniformed soldier, spontaneously knelt in the dirt with me. We humbled ourselves and interceded for the nation.

In the interaction with a few pastors that weekend there was an obvious excitement that a number of churches were working together to man the prayer tent and to pray for the nation together. They were seemingly thrilled that at least one good thing emerging out of the political turmoil was church unity. That was 2014. Fast-forward just three years to May 2017. I had the privilege of attending a combined churches prayer meeting for the nation in the Sports Palace in Kiev. The theme was taken from 2 Chronicles 7:14 'If my people, who are called by my name, will humble themselves and pray and seek my face and turn from their wicked ways, then I will hear from heaven, and I will forgive their sin and will heal their land'.

Over 8,000 people joined together in prayer and unity for three hours as bishops and pastors from every denomination and church union – orthodox, evangelical, catholic, charismatic, pentecostal and messianic Jewish - led us in prayers of repentance. It was an unexpected gift from

God to be present at such a momentous occasion. Only four months later 200,000 Christians gathered for a Praise and Thanksgiving rally on Maidan. The previous time that so many people had gathered on Independence Square was during the revolution in 2014. There is hope for Ukraine yet and I believe it is going to play a significant role in both Eastern and Western Europe.

Rich Heritage

On the occasion of my mother's 60th birthday in July 1988 she gave me and my sisters each a fifty-page handwritten 'Legacy for my children and grand-children' written over a period of three years. Maybe this sowed the initial seed in my heart to one day do the same– write up my memoirs to leave as a legacy for at least my children and grand-children. She sadly passed away at age seventy-seven with another seventeen years that she did not write anything about. Fortunately, we have fond memories of her during those years. The opening line of her memoirs is 'Silver and gold have I none – but a few memories, yes!'

She recalls how she remembers one specific Sunday morning at church when I was still a teenager. There was a particular word for people who felt called to work for God and I responded to be prayed for. She wrote, 'I gave you to the Lord that morning, and Praise God, I am thrilled at the way He called you and used you'. Thanks Mom! What a rich heritage.

Another major part of my spiritual heritage comes from my grandfather Bill or, more correctly, William Rufus Blake. We affectionately referred to him as 'Grampie' (for grandpa). He was born on 21 March 1901. His father, my great-grandfather Blake, had immigrated to South Africa from Ireland in the late nineteenth century and married Johanna Delport. Bill Blake married Evelyn May Curnick, whose grandfather in turn had immigrated to South Africa from Gloucestershire, England after missing the boat that his parents had sailed to the USA on.

Grampie had a sister, Kathleen, and a younger brother George. His mother Johanna died soon after giving birth to George. Kathleen and George were 'adopted' by different families, although they kept the name Blake, and Grampie was sent to an orphanage. It is not clear why Grampie's dad, my great-grandfather Blake, was not around at that time. I don't know if he had passed away by then or had abandoned the family or if there were other reasons. At the age of 14 Grampie started working in a trading store.

On the eve of his 21st birthday, he challenged God to prove His existence to him by 12 o'clock the next day. By noon on his birthday nothing had happened. He took his uncle's gun and went into a plantation nearby. He put the gun to his chest, told God how disappointed he was that nothing had happened, and that no one had showed up to talk to him. While squeezing the trigger, 'somebody' grabbed his arm, knocked the gun flying and the bullet narrowly missing him. There was nobody in sight. He ran back to his bedroom bewildered at what had happened and disconcerted at the failed suicide attempt.

In the meantime, God had spoken to a Mr van Tonder, a devoted Christian who lived miles away, to go to the third town across the river. In a remarkable way God led him to the specific homestead, arriving just shortly after Grampie had entered his bedroom. Mr van Tonder spent hours counselling him and praying with him. Shortly before midnight on his 21st birthday William Rufus Blake surrendered his life to the Lordship of Christ and became a devoted follower of Jesus.

Apart from owning and running trading stores Grampie also pastored a number of congregations. My mother recalls how they 'lived by faith' and saw God's incredible faithfulness to them as a family. She also told of seeing many supernatural healings and astonishing miracles through Grampie's ministry. He served with the Allied forces in Egypt as a medic in the Second World War. The only physical thing that I inherited from him is his 'Star of Africa' war medal. I treasure it.

Grampie became a widower just a few days after my birth. My grannie Evelyn May (Curnick) Blake had been chronically ill for months and when she received the telegram of my birth that my Mom and I were well she passed away without ever seeing me or my cousin Gordon who had been born a week earlier.

There were a number of years that Grampie lived in my parents' home. I regret not having had the foresight to pick his brain and glean a lot more information from him. For example, I don't even know what his father's first name was. Even my mother didn't know much about her grandfather except that he had emigrated from Ireland. I would have liked to hear more about Grampie's escapades during the war in Egypt. He apparently performed many post-mortems and minor operations. I would have loved to hear more about his adventures in ministry and have learned from his amazing experiences and relationship with God.

My mom tells of an occasion when he prayed for a lady who had swallowed a broken needle. She woke up in the middle of the night feeling her finger snagging on the sheet only to find the needle protruding from it. He loved open-air preaching. On one of these occasions he was confronted by a large man with a long dagger, raised ready to strike. He simply 'bound him in the name of Jesus' and continued his sermon. The man stood frozen in that position until he concluded his talk. At that point, the man fell in the dust and surrendered his life to Christ.

On another occasion, he was summoned to pray for a dying lady. When he eventually did arrive at the home she had already passed away. He often said that because of his Irish blood he always argued with God – especially about how to pray in challenging situations like this one. 'Why me?' and 'Why now?' and 'How?' He felt not to panic but to ask everyone to leave the room and to lay his pocket Bible on her clasped hands. As simple as that. When he did she opened her eyes stared at the wall and exclaimed 'It is so dirty here. Why did you bring me back? It was so pleasant with The Lord'. The lady continued to live for a few more years. In retrospect, I would have loved to talk to him more about such incidents and maybe have some of that faith and legacy rub off on me.

For a short period, we shared a room together divided by a rudimentary partition. Most nights I would hear him systematically pray for his two daughters and their husbands and all us grandchildren, by name. That is probably the greatest investment he made in our lives and I treasure that legacy.

oOo

Chapter 16
A Thumbnail Sketch of God

As for you, my son Solomon, know the God of your
father, and serve Him with a loyal heart and with
a willing mind; for the LORD searches all hearts
and understands all the intent of the thoughts.
If you seek Him, He will be found by you;
but if you forsake Him, He will cast
you off forever.
1 Chronicles 28:9 (NKJV)

Let not the wise boast of their wisdom or the strong
boast of their strength or the rich boast of their riches,
but let the one who boasts boast about this: that they
have the understanding to know me, that I am
the LORD, who exercises kindness, justice and
righteousness on earth, for in these I delight,
declares the LORD.
Jeremiah 9:23,24

Now this is eternal life: that they know you,
the only true God, and Jesus Christ,
whom you have sent.
John 17:3

The heavens declare the glory of God;
the skies proclaim the work of His hands.
Psalm 19:1

I am so pleased that God, although infinite, is knowable. He has chosen to reveal Himself to mankind through nature, the Bible, and ultimately in the person of Jesus Christ.

I realised to my embarrassment in 1973 that I didn't really have a clue about the true nature and character of God. I didn't know Him well enough to tell others about Him. I started on an exciting journey of discovery that continues to this day and will probably continue through all eternity. There is always more about our limitless God to be discovered and understood. Even the characteristics we do know about God have more facets and can be plumbed to greater depths.

In the 1980s I attended a conference in Indianapolis, USA with a group of YWAM leaders. During one of the worship sessions, Floyd McClung played a recording of a pastor extolling the virtues of who he knew God to be, using all the adjectives he could muster. I was deeply touched. Over the ensuing three decades I have been collating my own expression of who God is to me. God is infinitely greater than I can ever comprehend with my finite mind or express in one language with a limited vocabulary. Compared to all that He is, my attempt to explain him is infinitesimal – hence a 'thumbnail sketch' of God.

The Nature and Character of God

He is the uncreated Creator; the unlimited God of the universe who always existed. He is eternal. He is Alpha and Omega. He had no beginning and will have no end. He is from eternity to eternity and will exist forever and ever. He is personal and approachable yet infinite and unquantifiable. There is no other god beside Him. He is it.

He is fundamental reality, the most valuable being in the universe. He is Sovereign and Almighty. Omnipotent - all powerful; Omnipresent - everywhere present all at the same instant; and Omniscient - knowing everything that is knowable. He is astoundingly consistent. There is no contradiction in Him. He is immovable, unshakable, and unchangeable. He is the embodiment of a safe place. He can never not be near us.

He is Father, Son and Holy Spirit; three distinct personalities entirely united in essence and purpose in a Trinity of Being. He is supremely intelligent and interminably wise. He thinks, reasons, remembers, and even chooses to forget our sins and iniquities. He has the capacity to experience immeasurable emotion - the pinnacle of joy and the deepest agony of a broken heart – simultaneously.

He rejoices over us with singing and takes great pleasure and delight in those who reverently respect and obey Him. He grieves over sin and rebellion. He takes no pleasure in condemning the guilty. He feels no relief when people are lost for eternity. His heart is broken over the sin and the suffering in the world.

He is original and real. He originates His own actions. He pours Himself out lovingly for all of humanity and is willing the highest good for every single individual on earth. He always does what is right and good and loving and profitable for everyone. He is a benevolent God. He is LOVE.

He is unquestionably reliable, totally impartial, genuinely humble, completely trustworthy, and profoundly faithful. He is the personification of goodness. He is exceptionally kind, unswervingly gracious, abundantly merciful and as gentle as a dove. He is extravagantly generous, consistently forgiving, abounding in patience. He is excellent in all His ways, flawless in character, pristinely beautiful, and majestically holy. He is transparently pure and undeniably innocent. He has no faults, no wrong motives, and nothing lacking. He is perfect and just. He is righteous.

He has absolute authority and demands undivided allegiance, complete submission, and total worship. He is jealous for His name and will share His glory with no other. He is the wonderful counsellor, the mighty God, the prince of peace, the supreme commander, the captain of the hosts of heaven and the most loving governor. His government of peace shall continue increasing throughout all eternity.

All things pure and holy and beautiful emanate from Him. Nothing exists without Him. All art originates with Him. He is the most detailed designer, the most exquisite choreographer, the most prolific songwriter, the incarnational communicator, and the grandest of sculptors. He is the original composer, the most colourful artist, and the most energetic of dancers.

He is known as Elohim (a plural noun) – expressing covenant relationships within one God; Jehovah – The Lord; El Shaddai – God Almighty; El Elyon – The Exalted One or The Most High God; El Olam – The Everlasting God; Adonai – My Lord; Kadesh - The Holy One; Abhir - The Mighty One and Caddik - The Righteous One. He is also known as Eloah and Yahweh.

He is Jehovah-Jireh - My Provider; Jehovah-Nissi - The Lord My Banner; Jehovah-Shammah - The Present Lord; Jehovah-Shalom - My Peace; Jehovah-Tsidkenu - Our Righteousness; Jehovah-Sabaoth - The Lord of Hosts. He is The Great I AM.

He is Abba, an astoundingly compassionate and caring father. He is father of the fatherless and the protector of the widows. He is exceedingly concerned for our well-being and is dedicated to intimate relationship with us. He longs for fellowship and communion with us. He gives meaning, identity, and a sense of value and worth to our lives. He is a place of safety and security. A refuge for the oppressed, a stronghold in times of anxiety. A fortress, a rock and a solid foundation. A hiding place in times of trouble. He is the paraclete, the comforter. A friend who sticks closer than a brother. He will never leave us nor forsake us.

He is the way, the truth, and the life. The champion of our souls. His name is a high tower, the righteous run into it and are safe. His life is the light of the world. He is the fountain of living water, the bread of life, the door, the good shepherd, the lily of the valley, the rose of Sharon, the lion of Judah, and the bright morning star. He is a cloud by day and a pillar of fire by night. He is really amazing!

He is the great physician. The anointed one. The healer of mind, soul, and body. He brings good news to the poor; binds up the broken hearted; proclaims freedom to the captives; comforts those who mourn; and releases prisoners from darkness. He gives beauty in exchange for ashes; oil of gladness instead of mourning; a garment of praise for a spirit of heaviness. He restores, redeems, and replaces what the enemy has devoured. He is a servant king.

He is the king of kings, the lord of lords and the only true God. His name is above every name. The Lord most high. The majestic one. He is our warrior king, the victorious one, the rider on the white horse who is called Faithful and True. He is the liberator, the burden bearer, the yoke destroyer, the bondage breaker, and the promise keeper. He honours His covenants. He is simply awesome.

He is the high priest, the good shepherd, the bridegroom, the head of the Church and the lover of my soul. He is the Passover lamb, the supreme sacrifice. He died and rose again. He is the resurrection and the life. HE IS THE CHRIST, THE SON OF THE LIVING GOD. HE IS JESUS!

He is the first-born of many, the prototype of us all. He is the revelation of the Father and the example of who we really are. He is our righteousness. He is Messiah the soon-coming king.

OH! I WISH I COULD DESCRIBE HIM TO YOU!

oOo

Epilogue

Regrets? Yes! I do have some. There are things I wish I hadn't done and other things I should have done but never got around to them before it was too late. However, I have no qualms about God and His call upon my life. He did know best and still does. I am more than content with the way my life has panned out and incredibly grateful for the guiding and protecting hand of God upon Cecilia and me since we got together as teenagers.

What next?

I am more motivated and passionate about serving the purposes of God in the world than I have ever been. He is undoubtedly at work on earth and I look forward to joining Him in what He is doing, wherever and whenever He would allow me to do so. I have no reason to doubt that the same God that has loved us greatly and provided for us over many years will continue to do so for the rest of our journey. He is trustworthy. I intend to keep trusting Him!

And You?

I trust that what I have shared from my life has encouraged you to get to know God for yourself and to be freed from the encumbrances of inferiority, comparison, and the opinions of others. You have been created on purpose, by a loving God, for a specific purpose. You are not an accident or mistake. May you discover that purpose and pursue it with a passion. Be real and allow the God who resides in you to be His own glorious self within you to make a difference in this world through you.

oOo

27384314R00144

Printed in Great Britain
by Amazon